FOR ORGANS, PIANOS & ELECTRONIC KEYBOARDS

12

DANCEABLE FAVORITES
2ND EDITION

Y0-EBA-442

ISBN 0-7935-4976-0

7777 W. Bluemound Rd. P.O. Box 13819 Milwaukee, WI 53213

E-Z Play ® Today Music Notation © 1975 by HAL LEONARD CORPORATION
E-Z PLAY and EASY ELECTRONIC KEYBOARD MUSIC are registered trademarks of HAL LEONARD CORPORATION.

For all works contained herein:
Unauthorized copying, arranging, adapting, recording or public performance is an infringement of copyright.
Infringers are liable under the law.

Visit Hal Leonard Online at
www.halleonard.com

FOR ORGANS, PIANOS & ELECTRONIC KEYBOARDS

12

DANCEABLE FAVORITES
2ND EDITION

CONTENTS

4	Aquellos Ojos Verdes (Green Eyes)
10	Baby Love
6	Beer Barrel Polka (Roll Out the Barrel)
13	Blame It on the Bossa Nova
16	Brazil
22	Ciribiribin
18	Cuanto Le Gusta
25	Dancing in the Street
28	Fly Me to the Moon
30	Goodnight, Sweetheart, Goodnight
32	The Great Pretender
35	In the Mood
38	The Loco-Motion
40	The Look of Love
42	L-O-V-E
44	Mambo #5
50	Shake, Rattle and Roll
47	Spanish Eyes
52	A String of Pearls
54	Tennessee Waltz
56	Twilight Time
58	The Twist
60	Where the Boys Are
63	REGISTRATION GUIDE

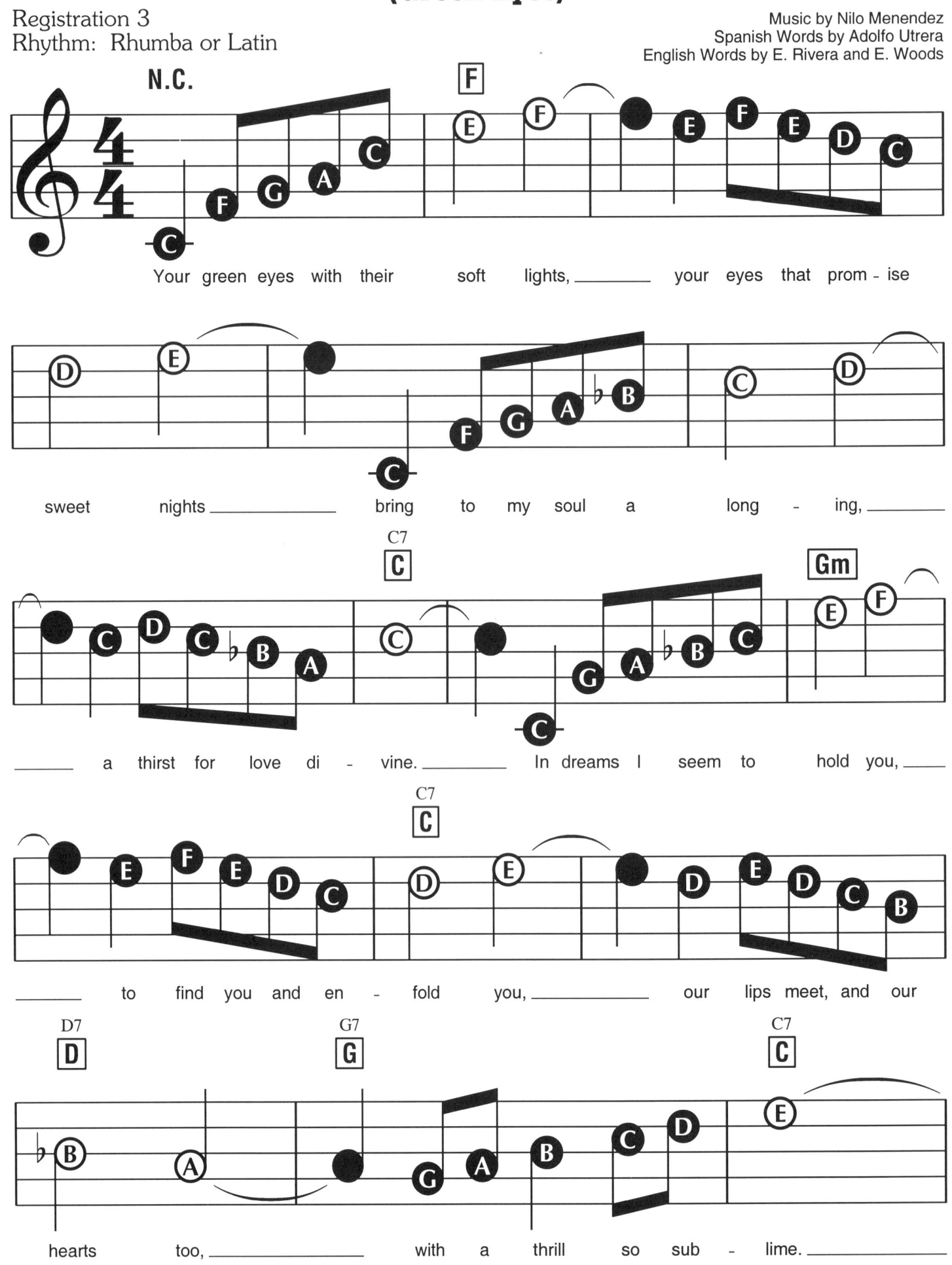

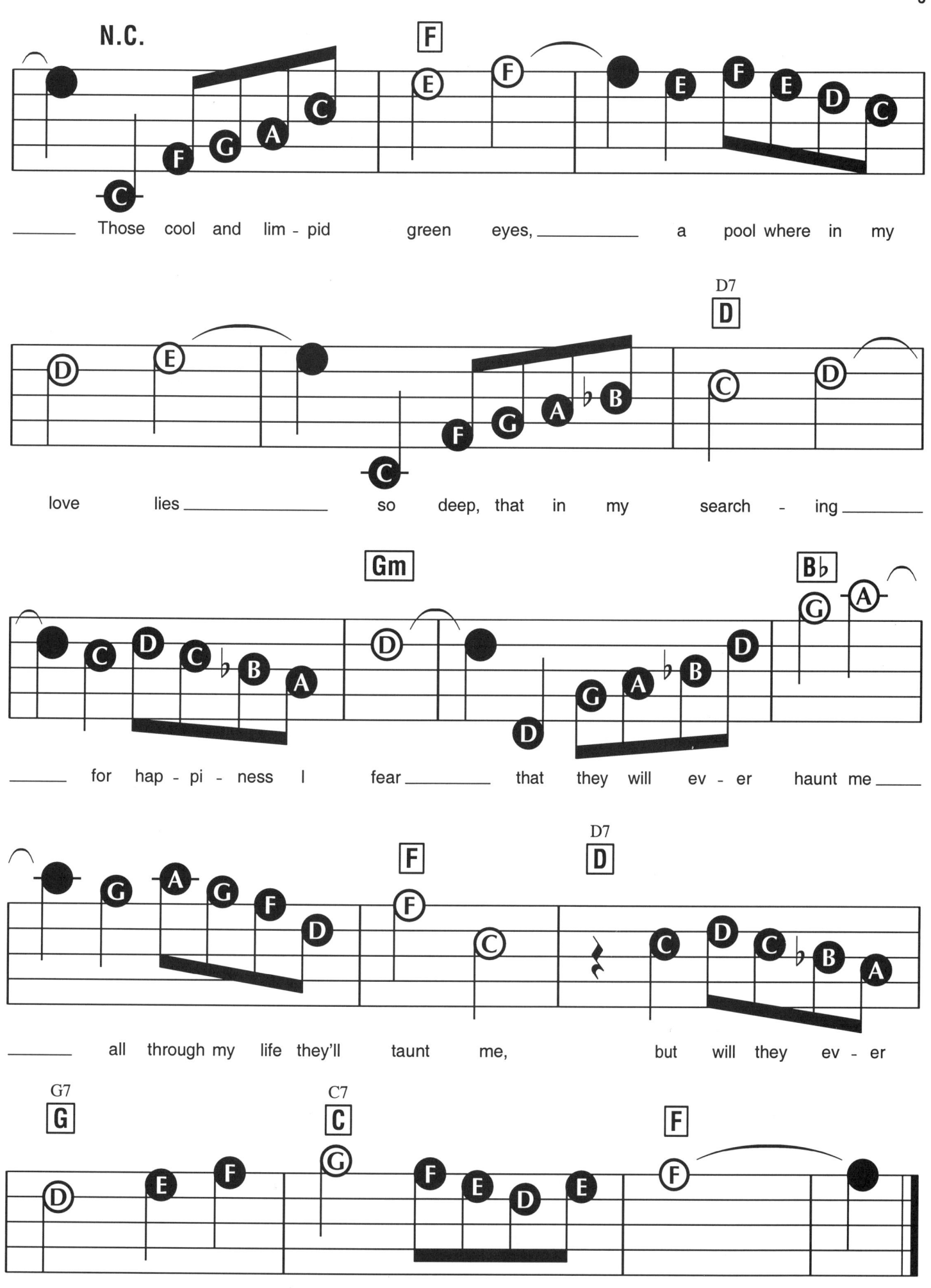

6

Beer Barrel Polka
(Roll Out the Barrel)
Based on the European success "Skoda Lasky"*

Registration 5
Rhythm: Polka or March

By Lew Brown, Wladimir A. Timm,
Jaromir Vejvoda and Vasek Zeman

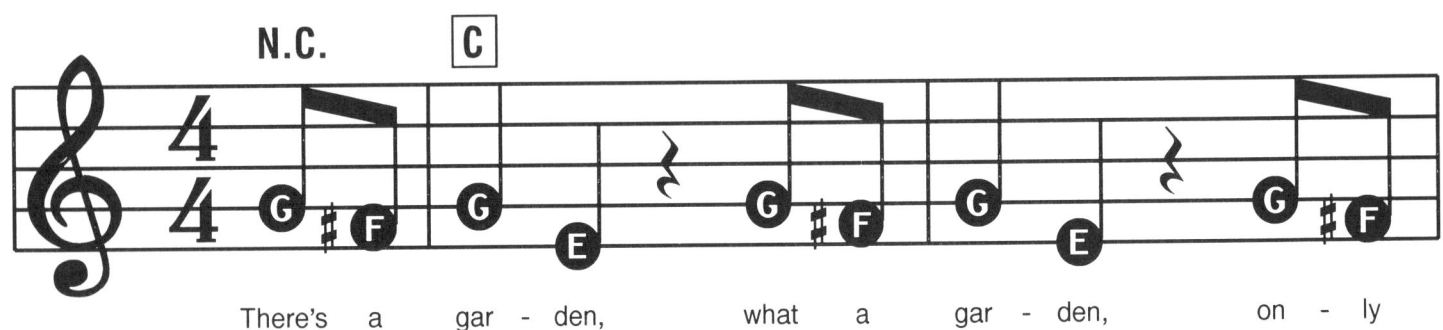

There's a gar - den, what a gar - den, on - ly

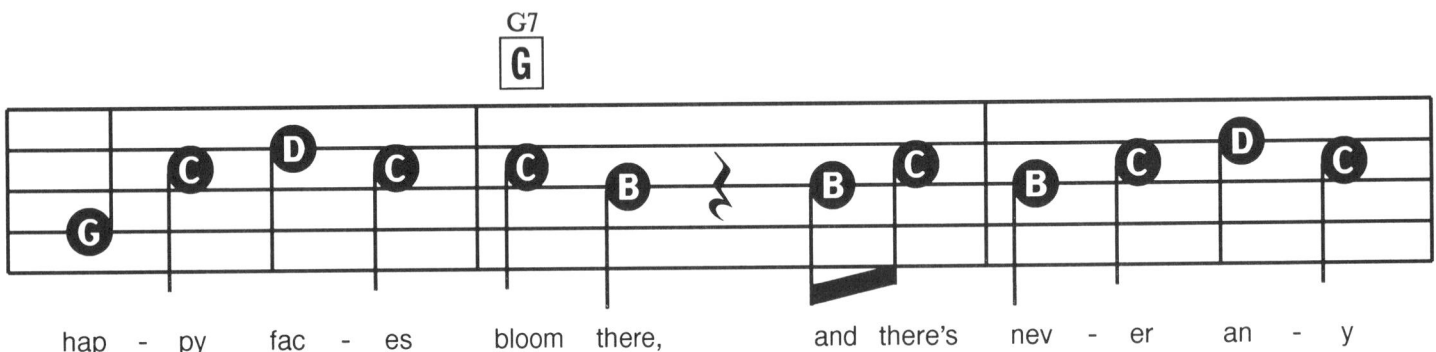

hap - py fac - es bloom there, and there's nev - er an - y

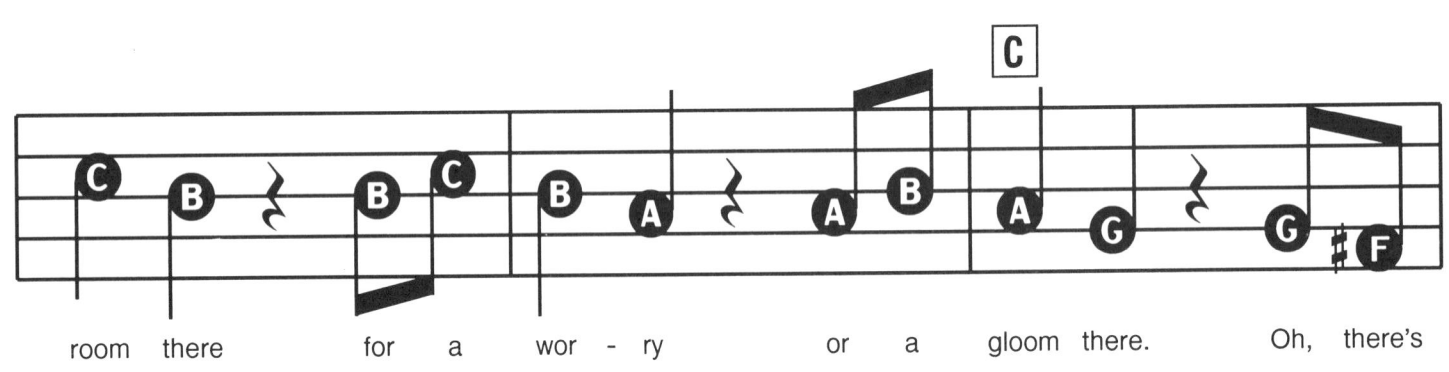

room there for a wor - ry or a gloom there. Oh, there's

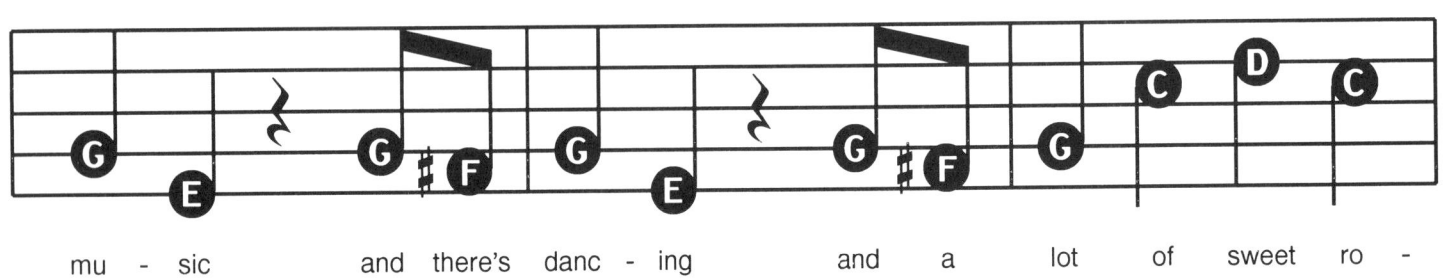

mu - sic and there's danc - ing and a lot of sweet ro -

*"Skoda Lasky" Copyright © 1934 Shapiro, Bernstein & Co., Inc., New York
Copyright Renewed
Copyright © 1939 Shapiro, Bernstein & Co., Inc., New York
Copyright Renewed
International Copyright Secured   All Rights Reserved
Used by Permission

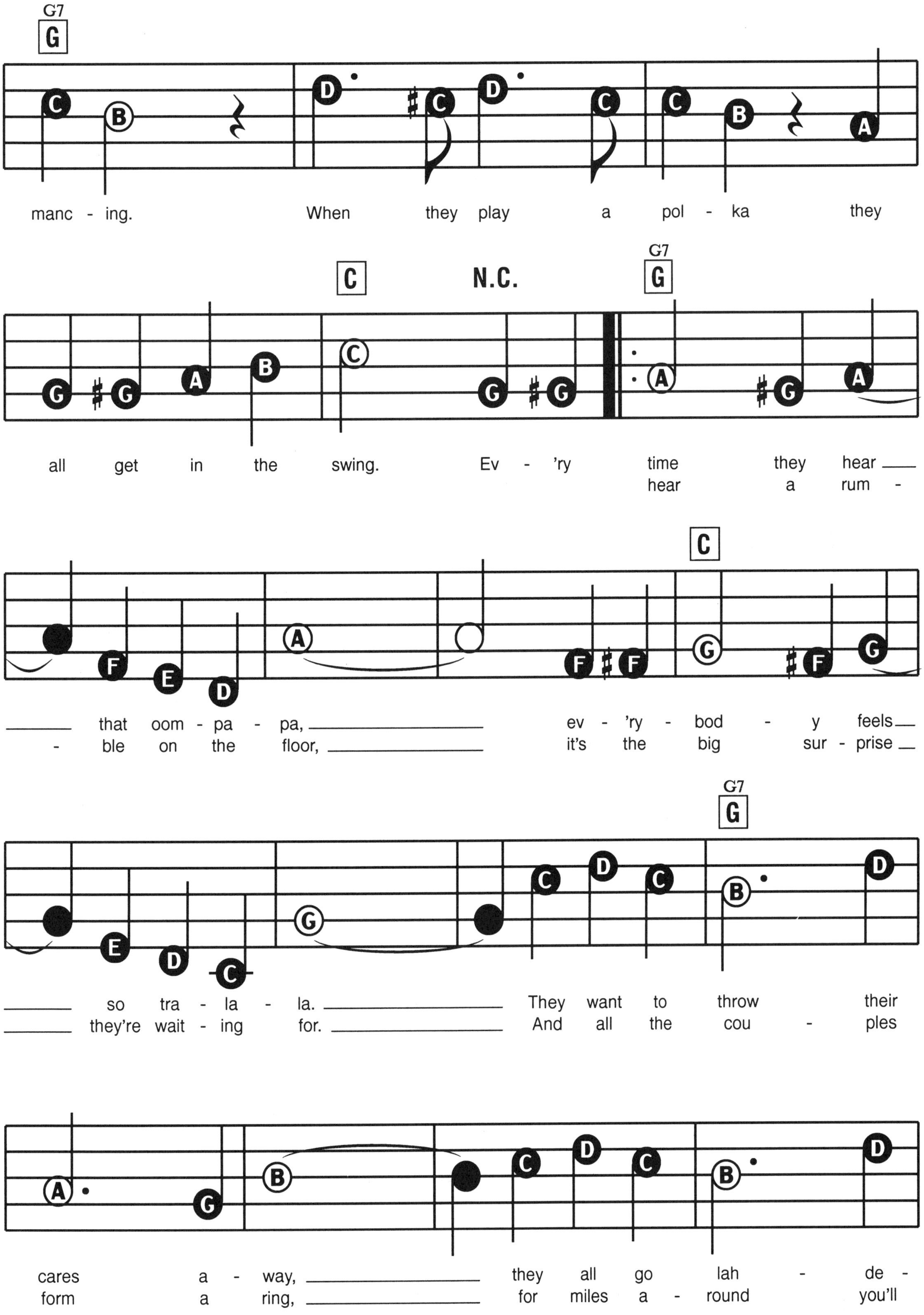

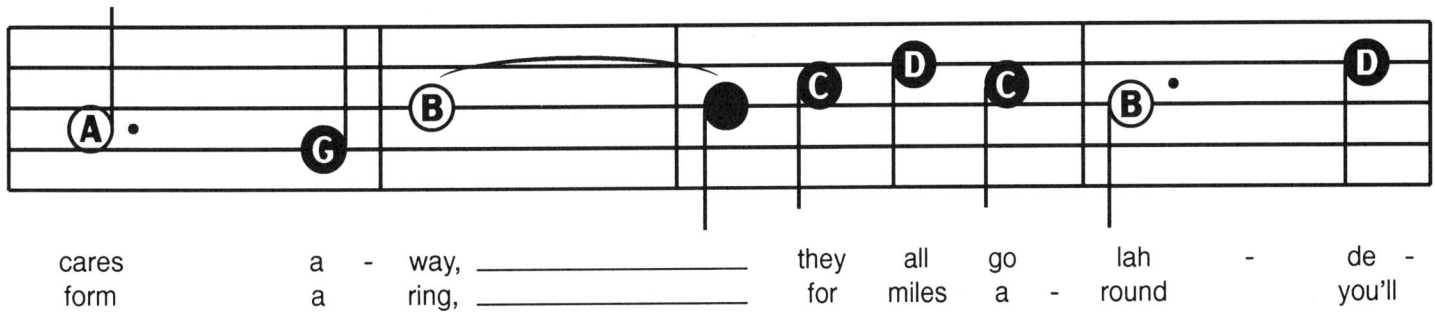

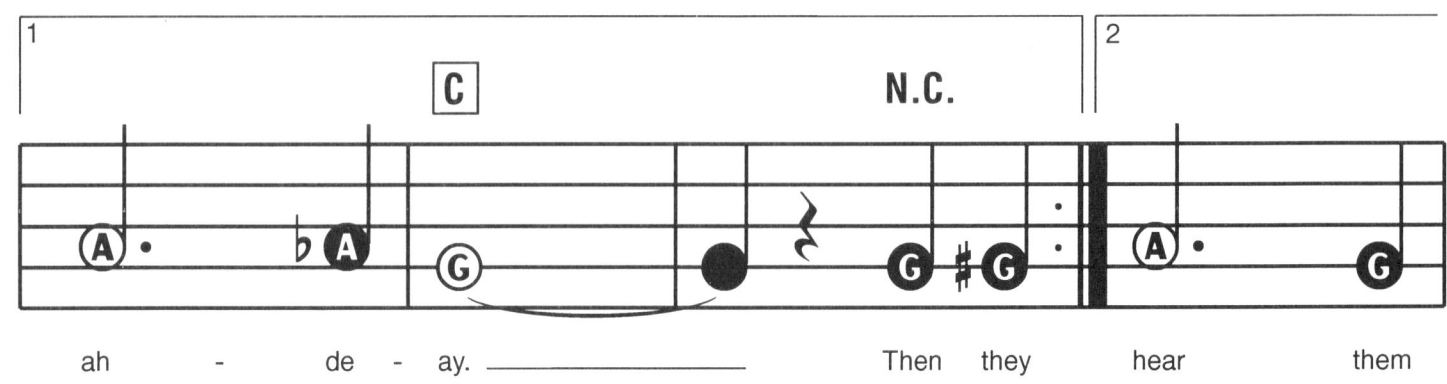
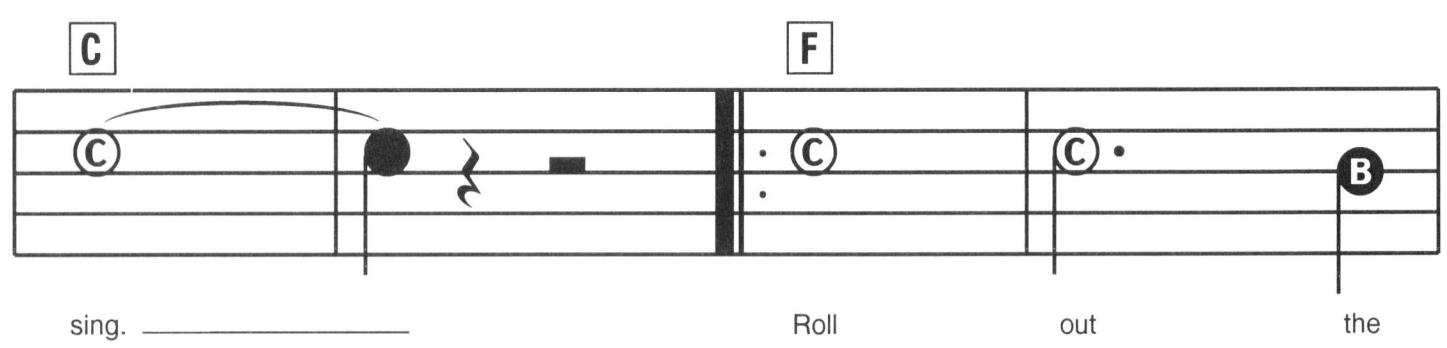
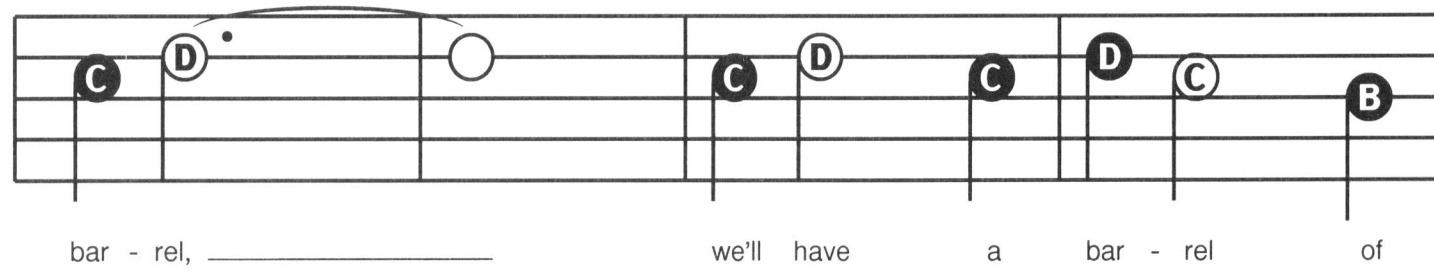
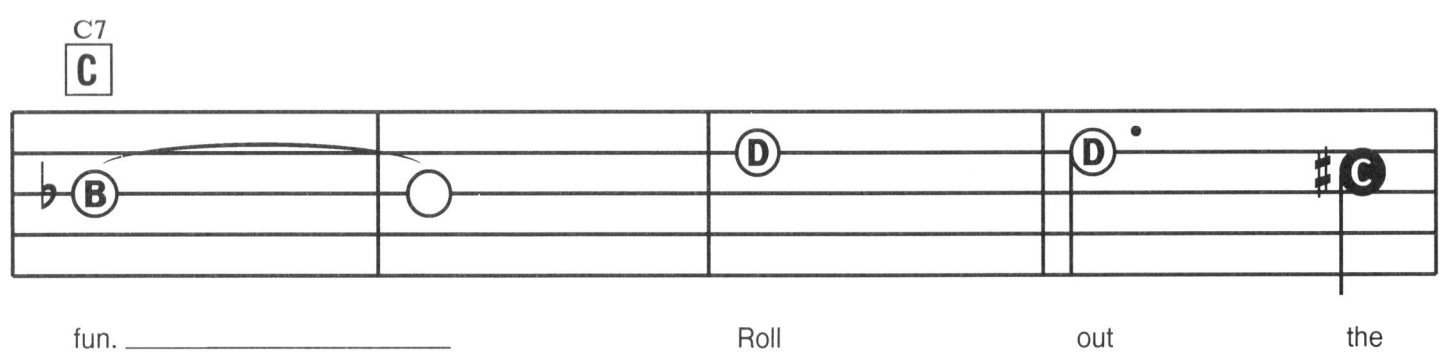
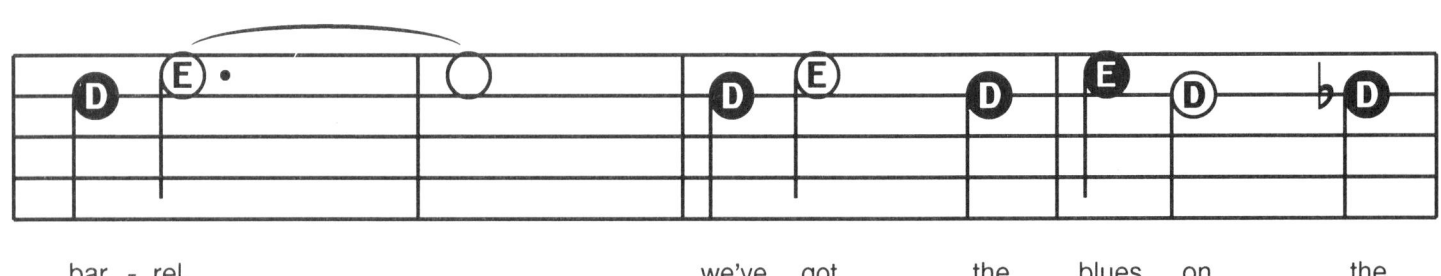

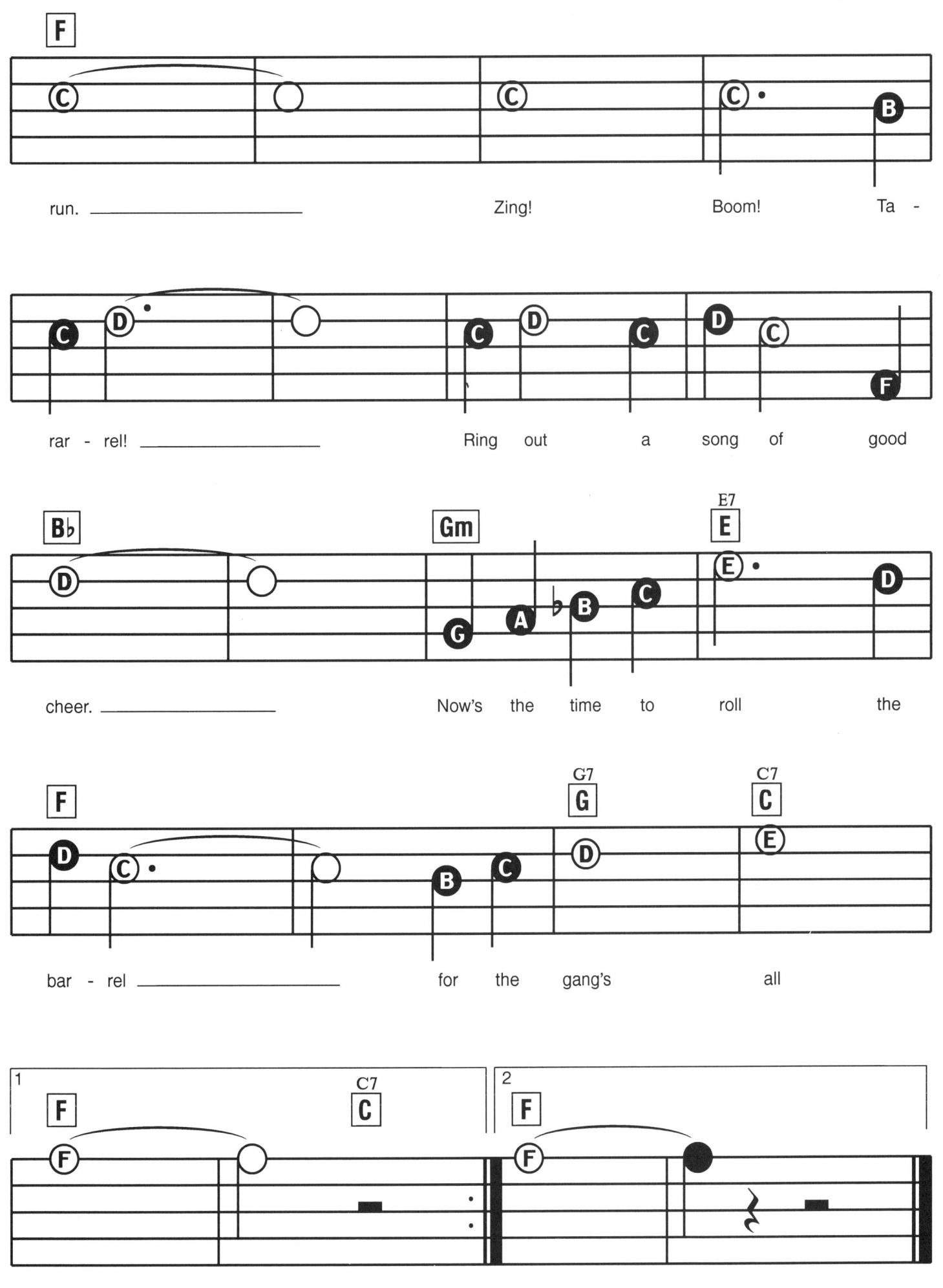

Baby Love

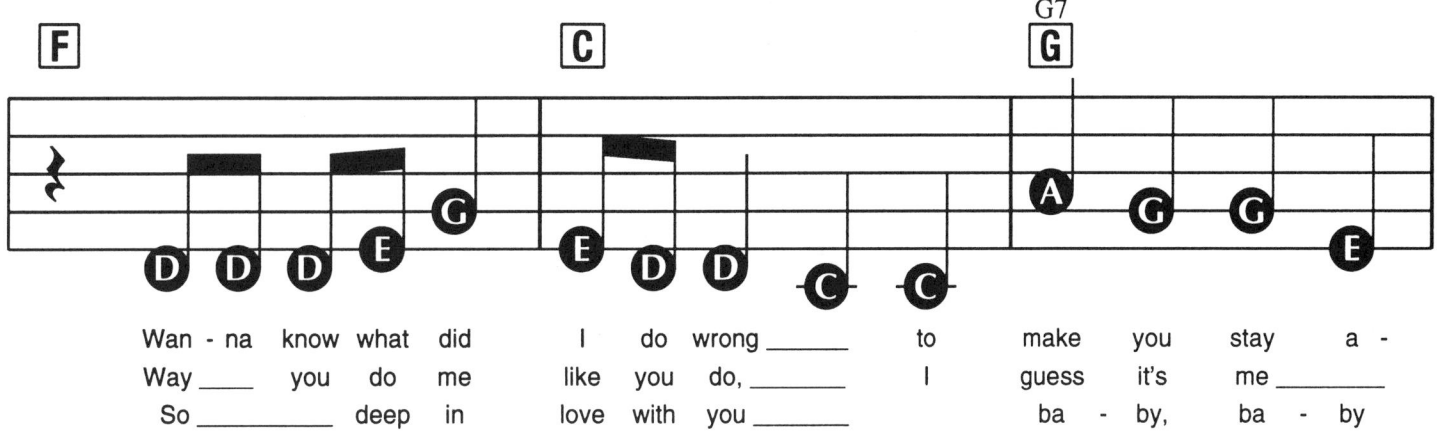
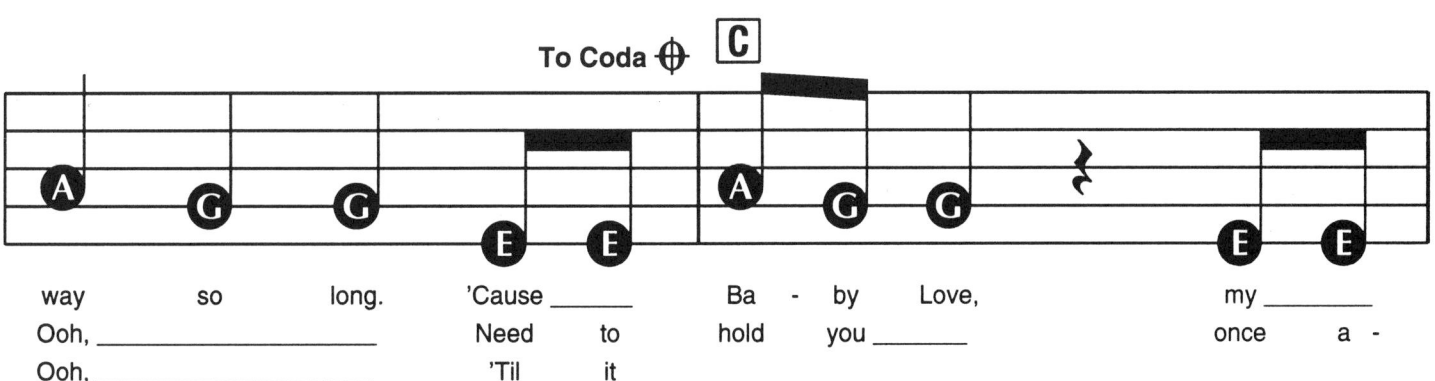
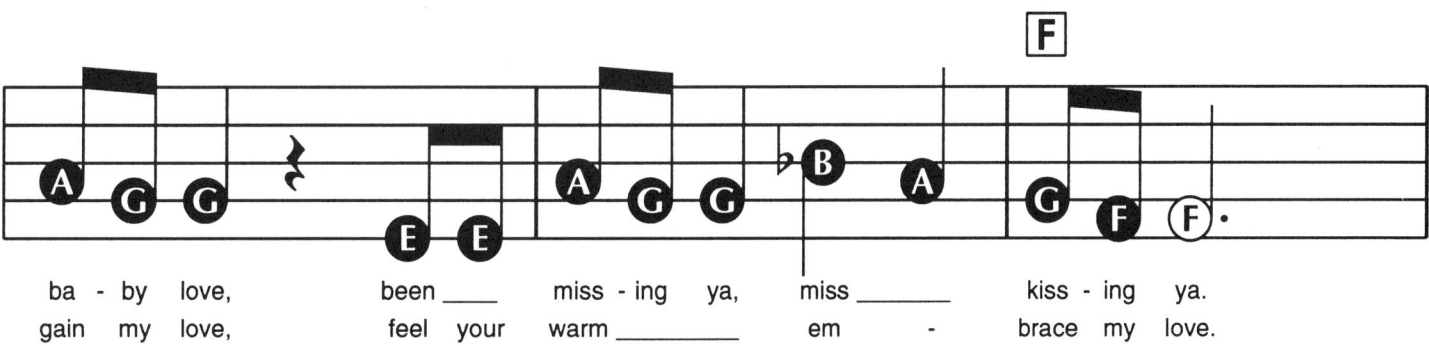
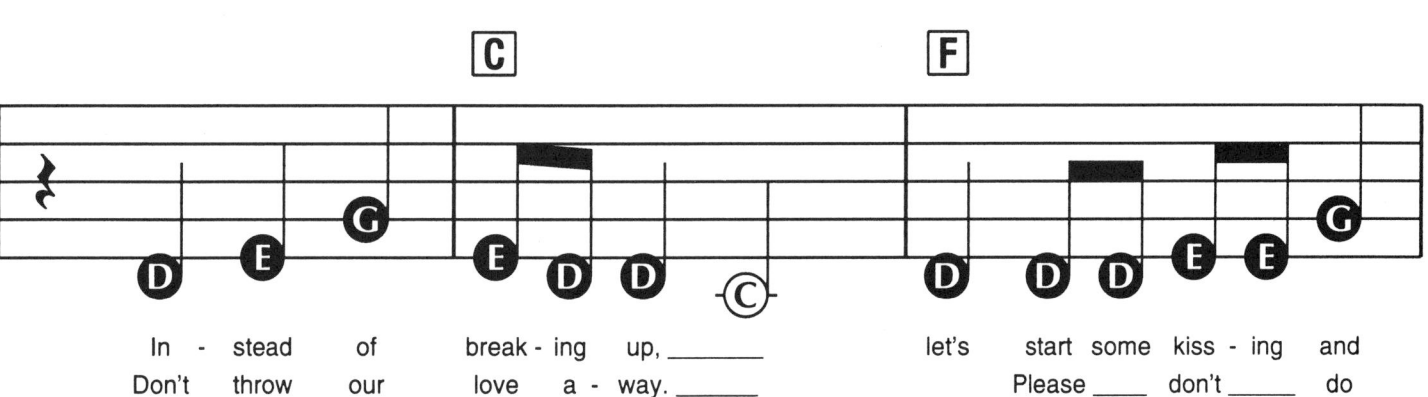

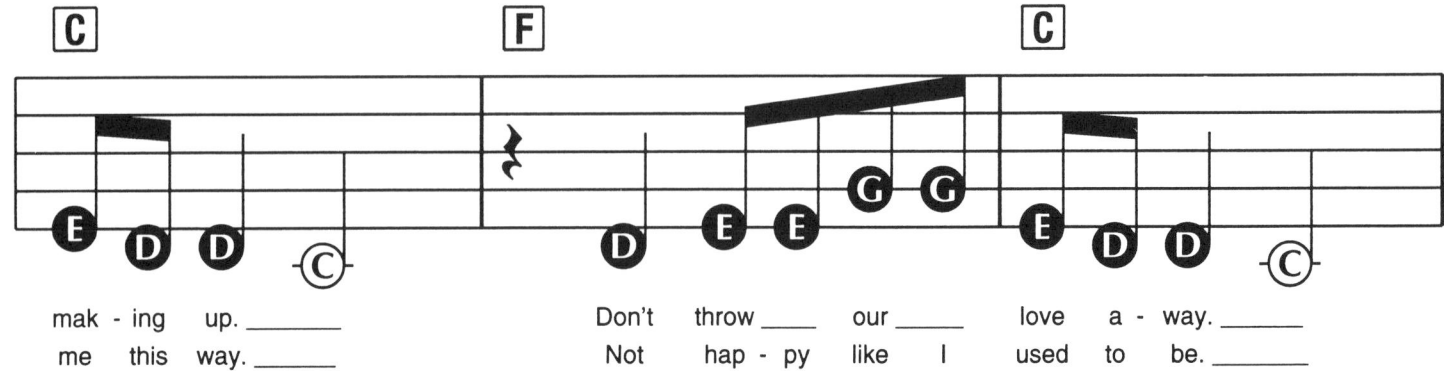
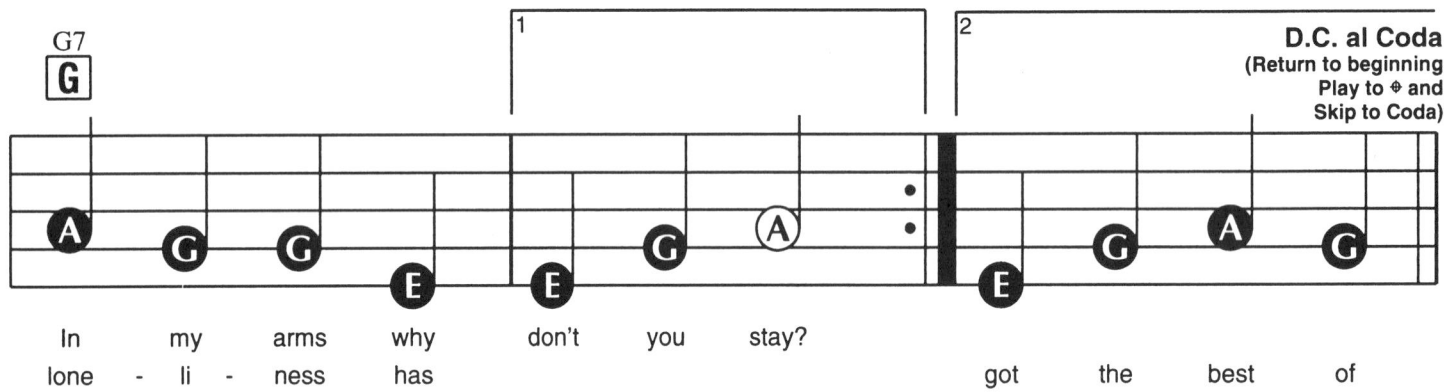
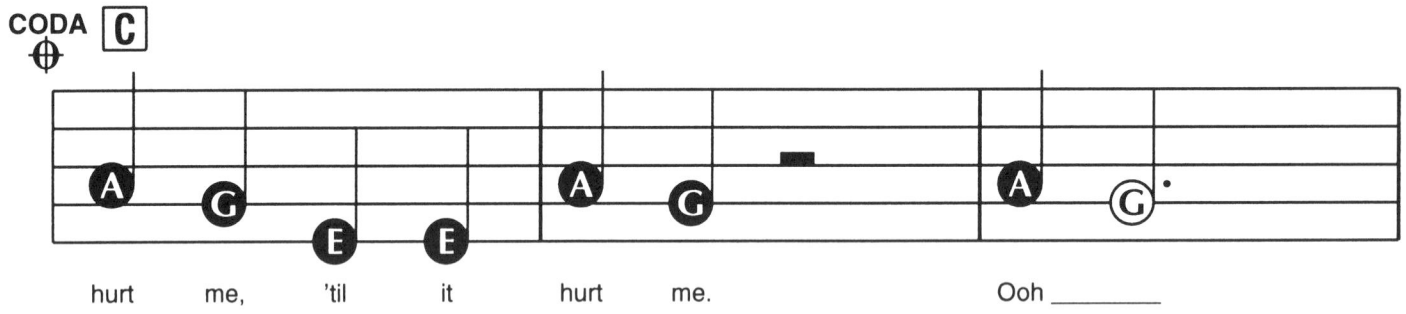
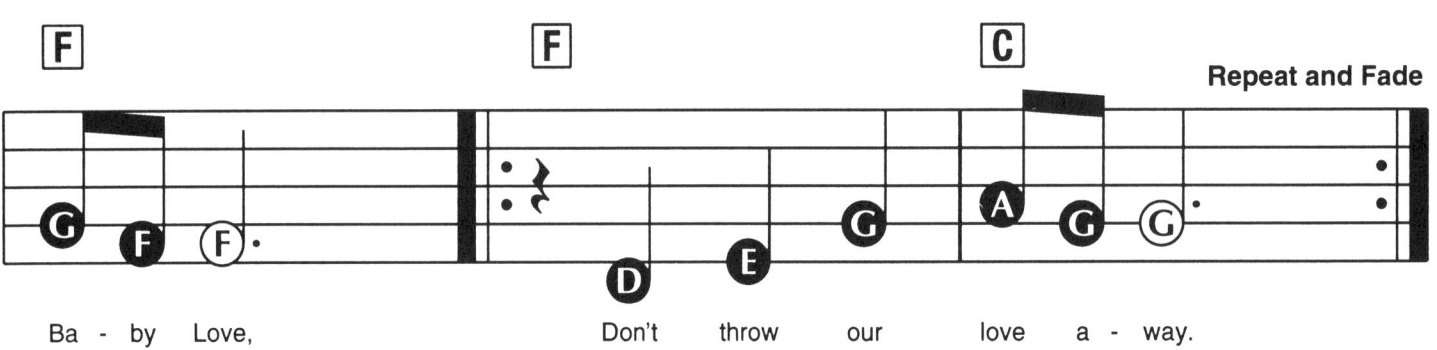

Blame It on the Bossa Nova

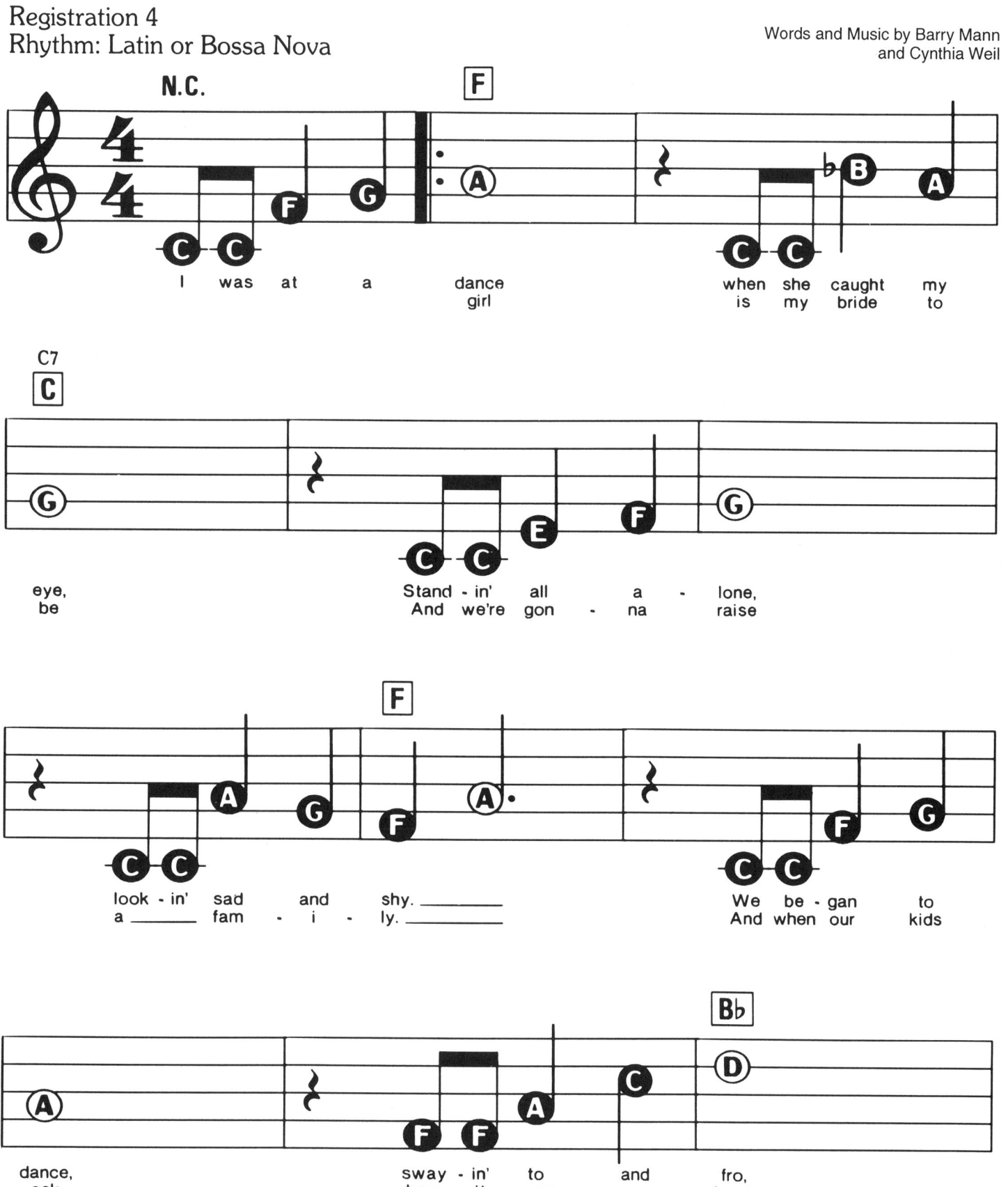

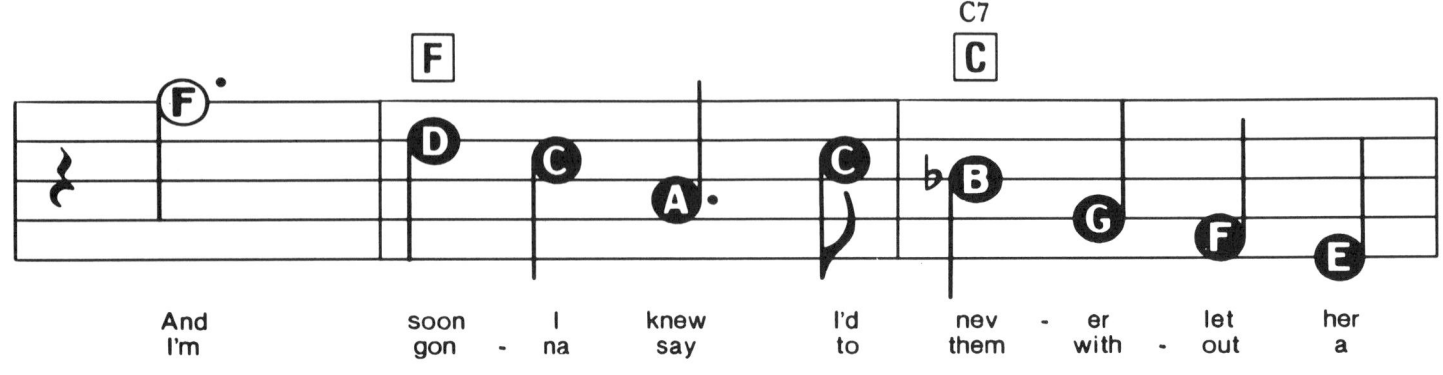
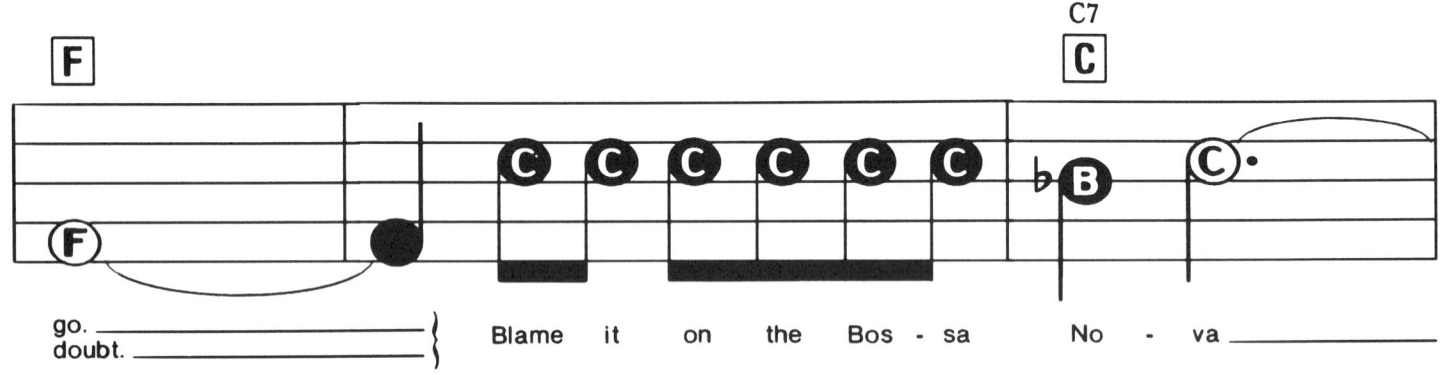
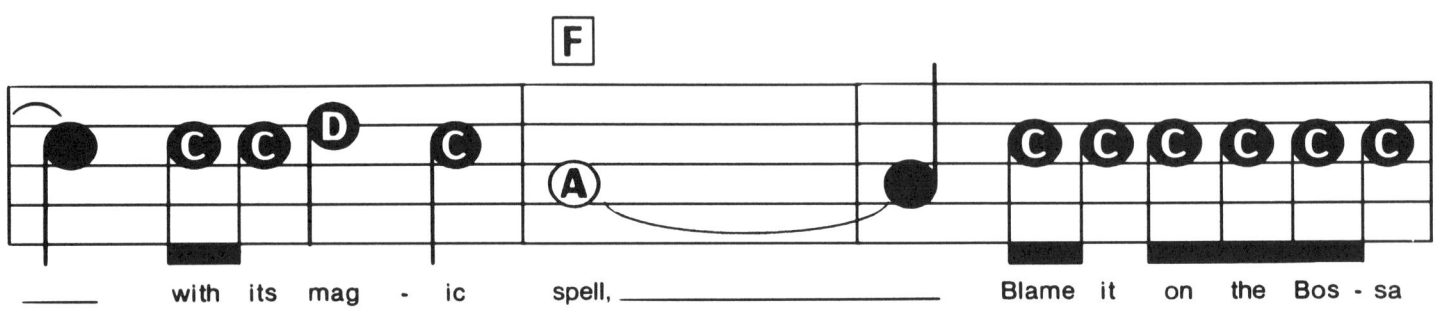
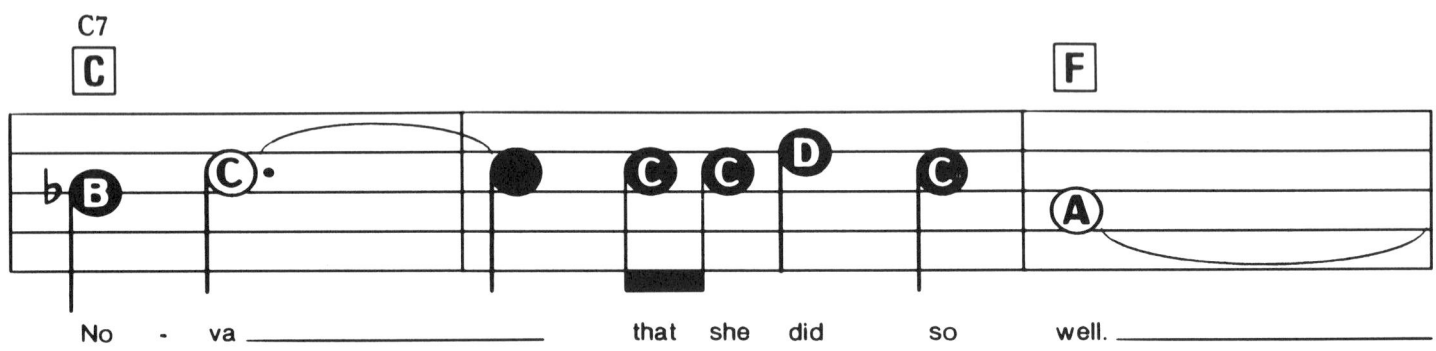
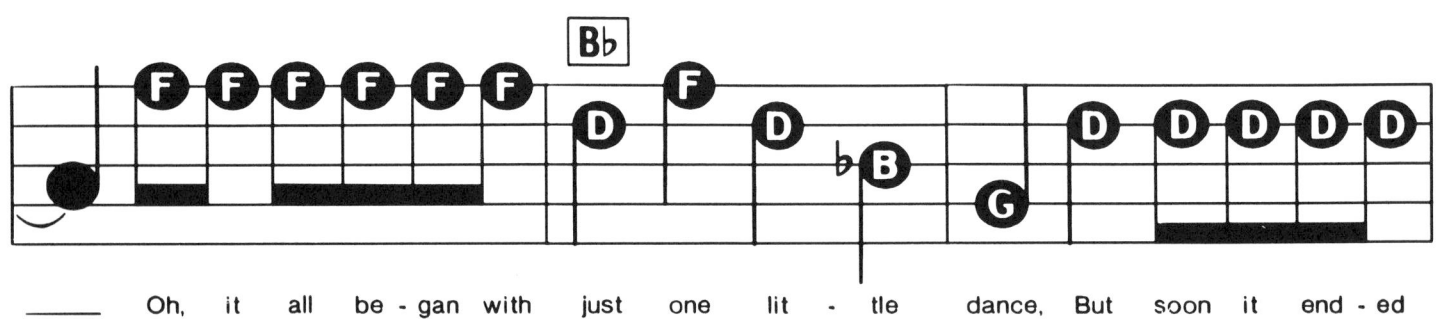

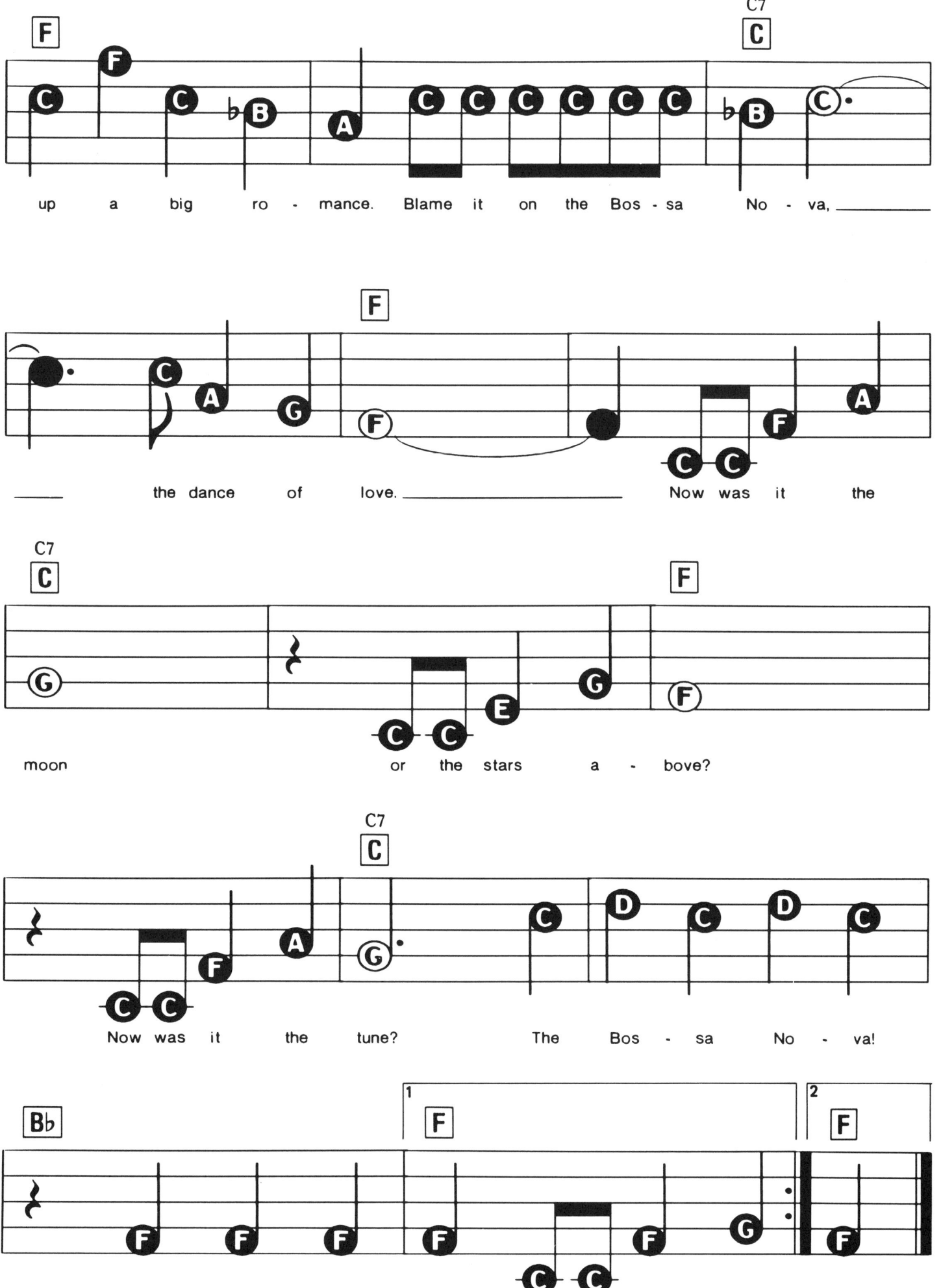

16

Brazil

Registration 4
Rhythm: Samba or Latin

Words and Music by S.K. Russell
and Ary Barroso

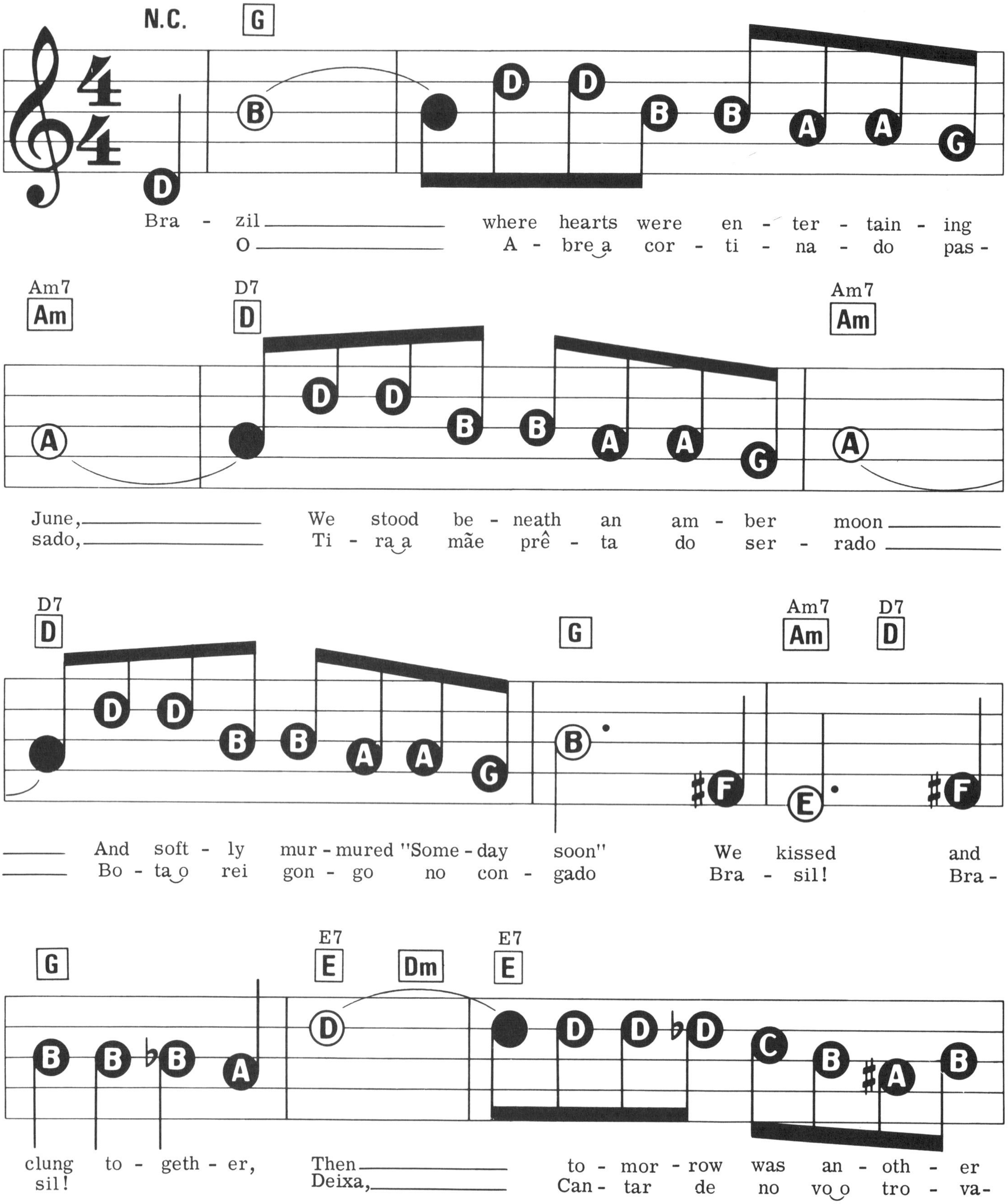

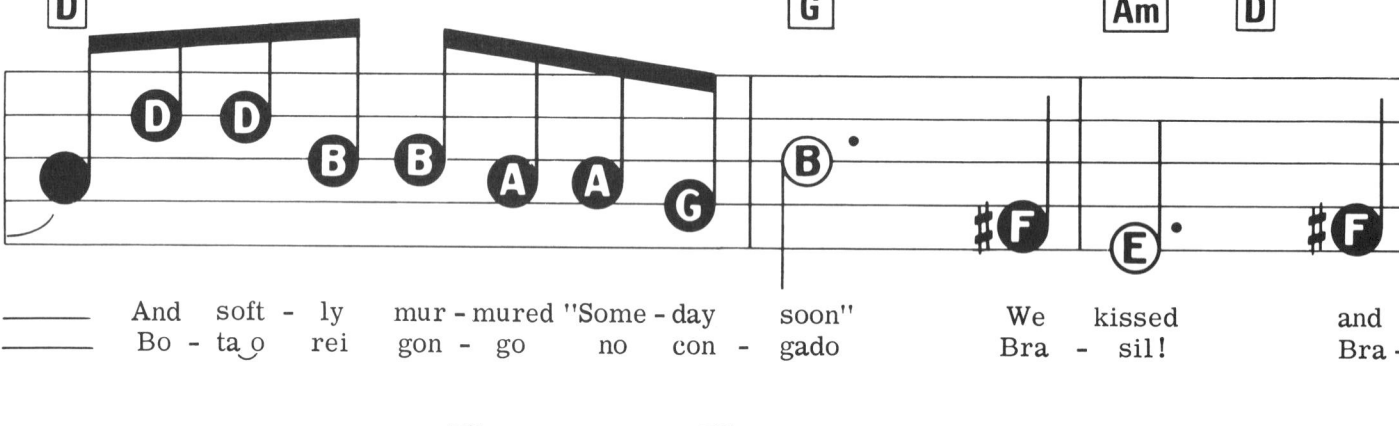

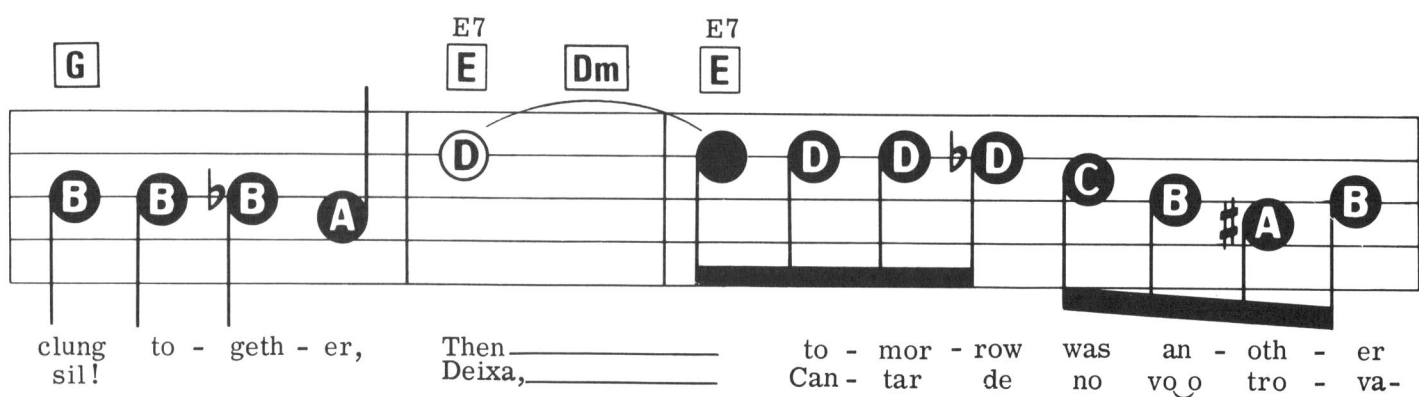

Copyright © 1941 by Peer International Corporation
Copyright Renewed
International Copyright Secured   All Rights Reserved

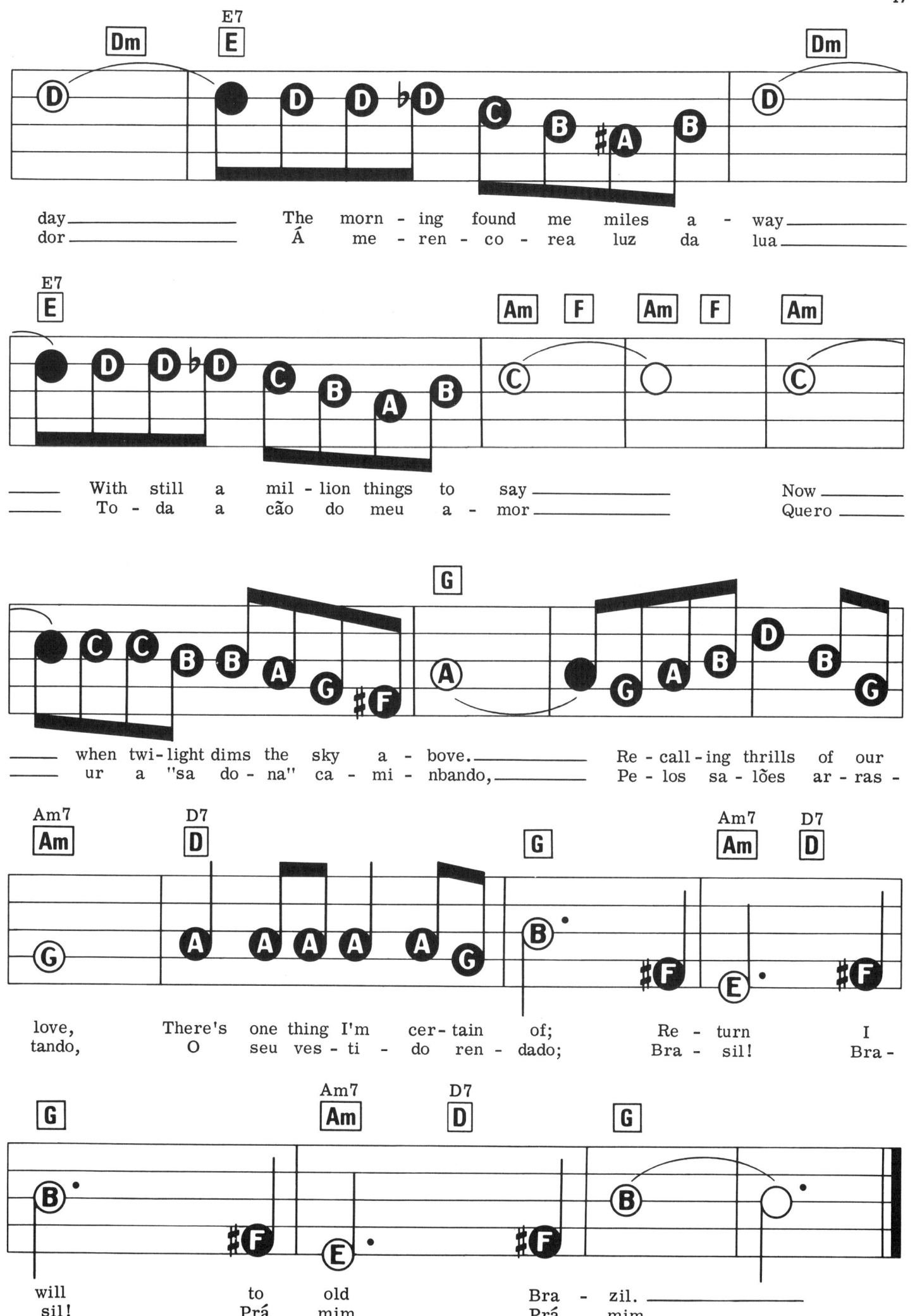

Cuanto Le Gusta

Registration 6
Rhythm: Swing or Fox Trot

Original Words and Music by Gabriel Ruiz
English Words by Ray Gilbert

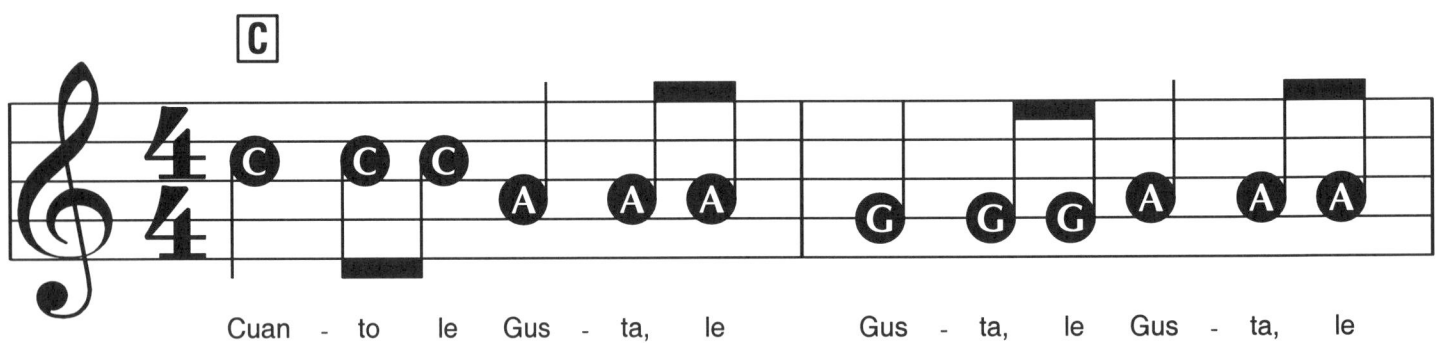
Cuan - to le Gus - ta, le Gus - ta, le Gus - ta, le

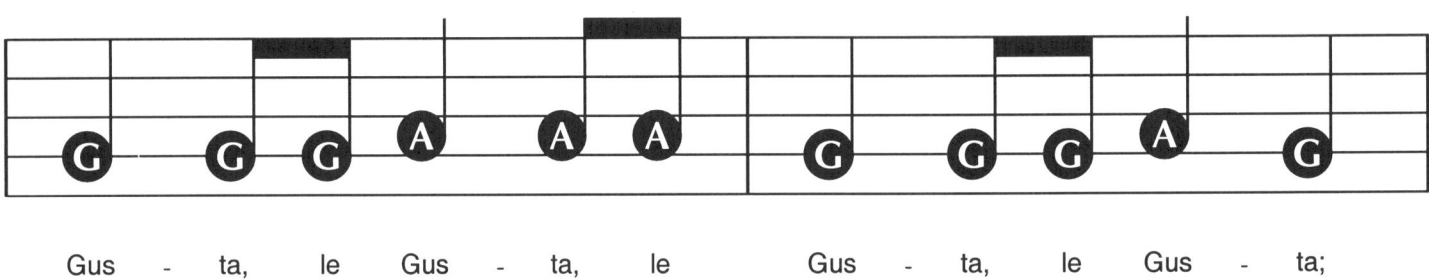
Gus - ta, le Gus - ta, le Gus - ta, le Gus - ta;

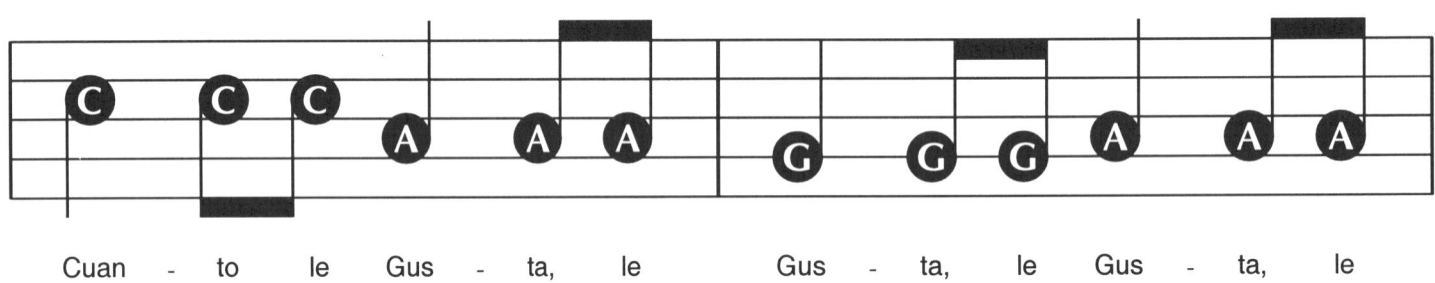
Cuan - to le Gus - ta, le Gus - ta, le Gus - ta, le

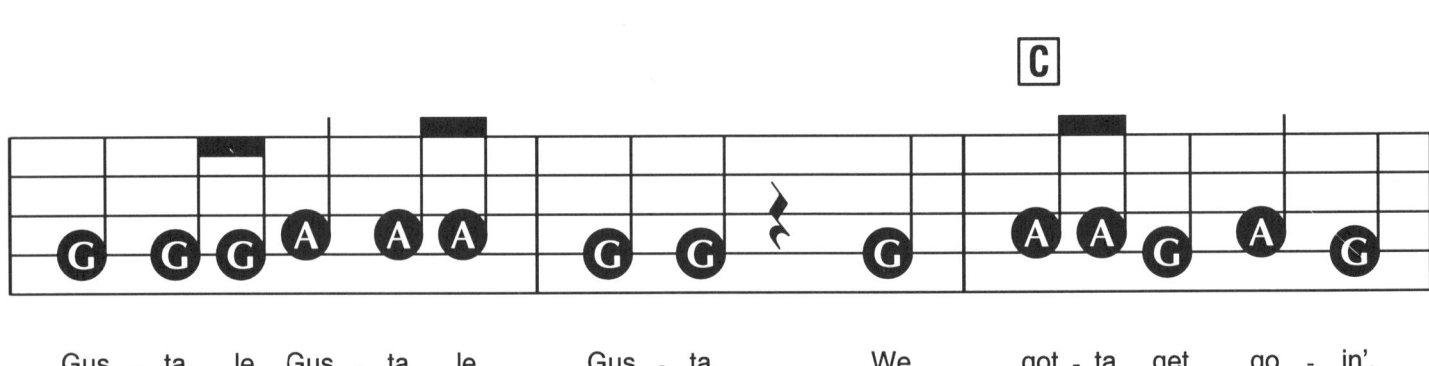
Gus - ta, le Gus - ta, le Gus - ta. We got - ta get go - in',

Copyright © 1948 by Peer International Corporation
Copyright Renewed
International Copyright Secured   All Rights Reserved

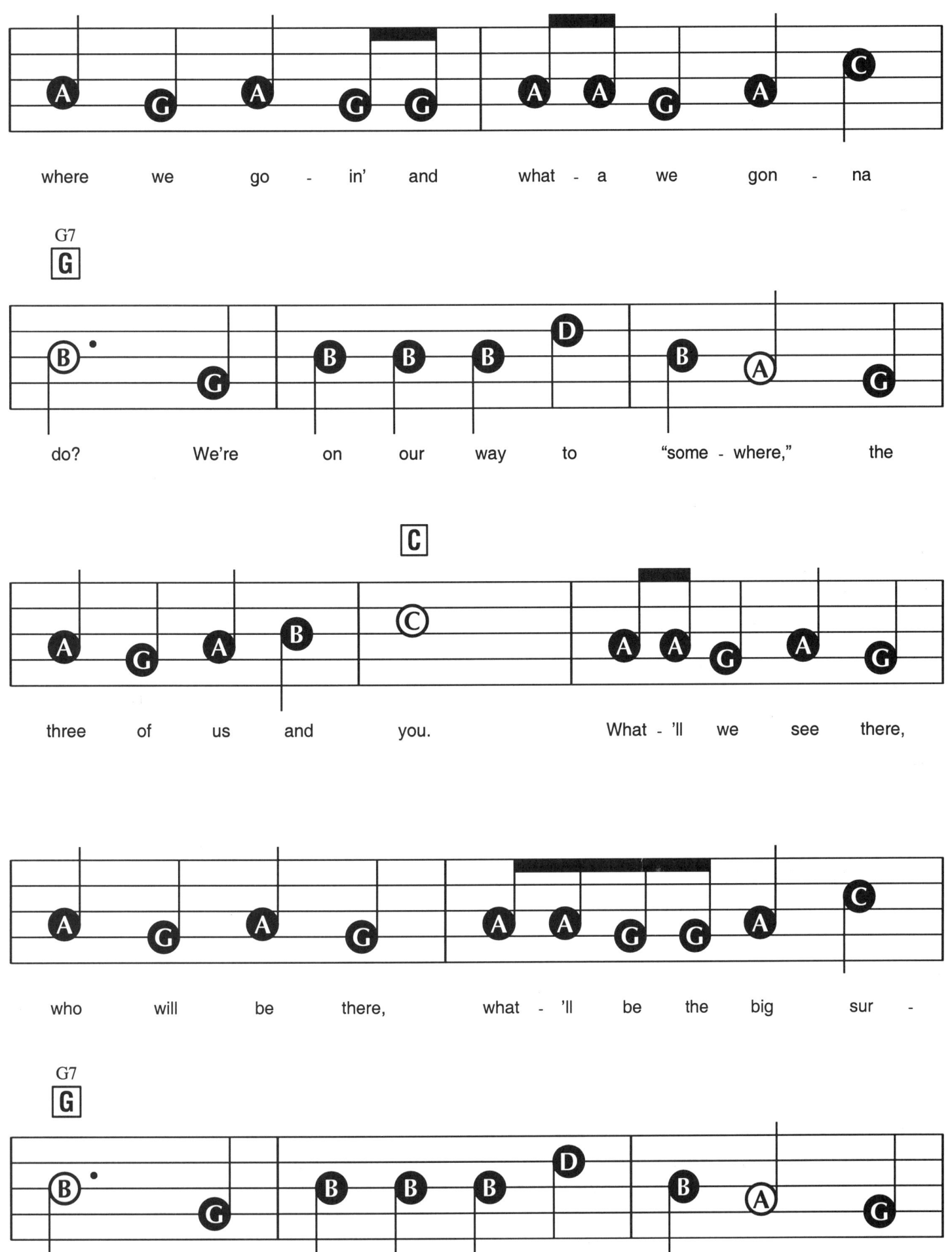

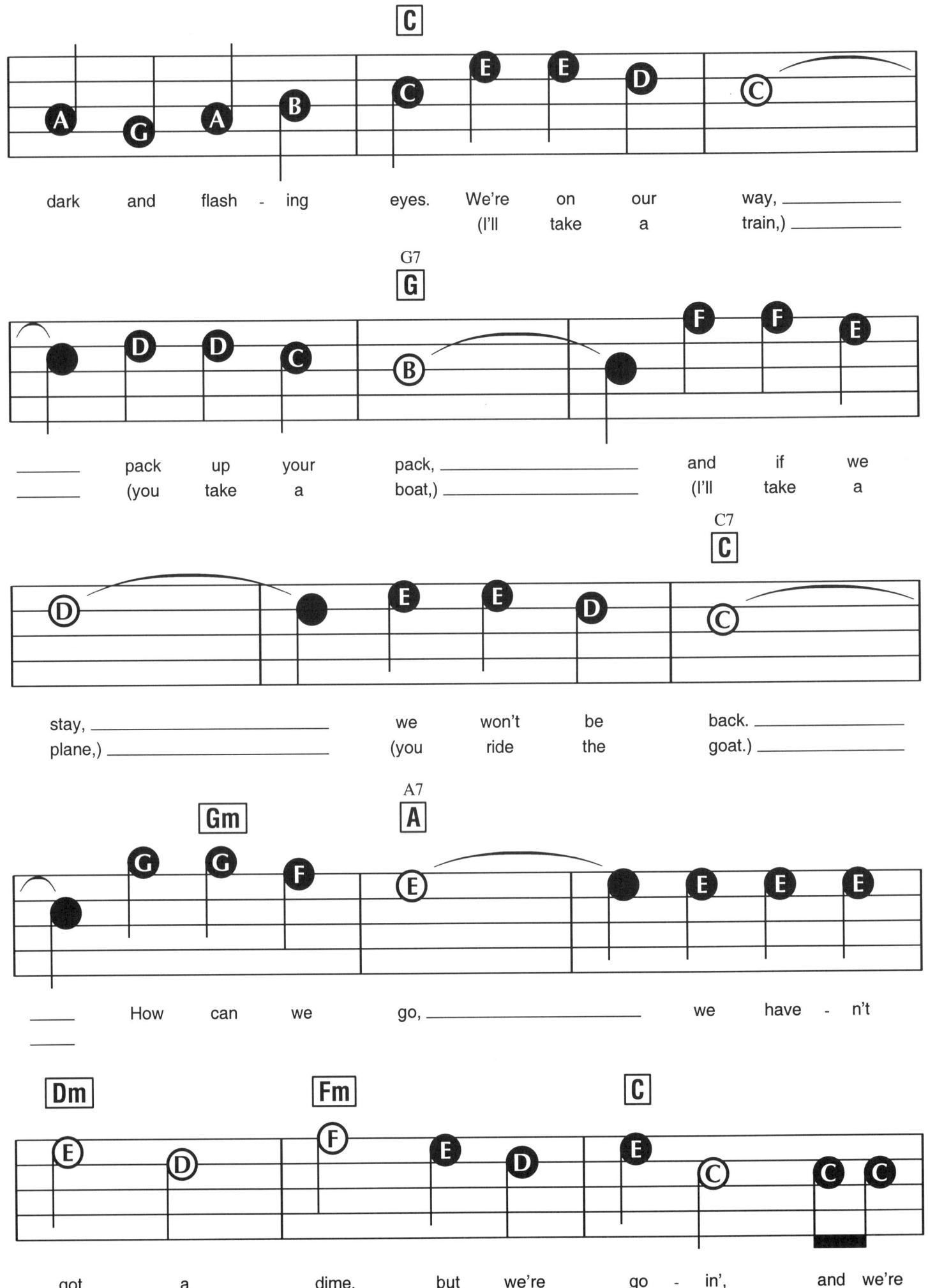

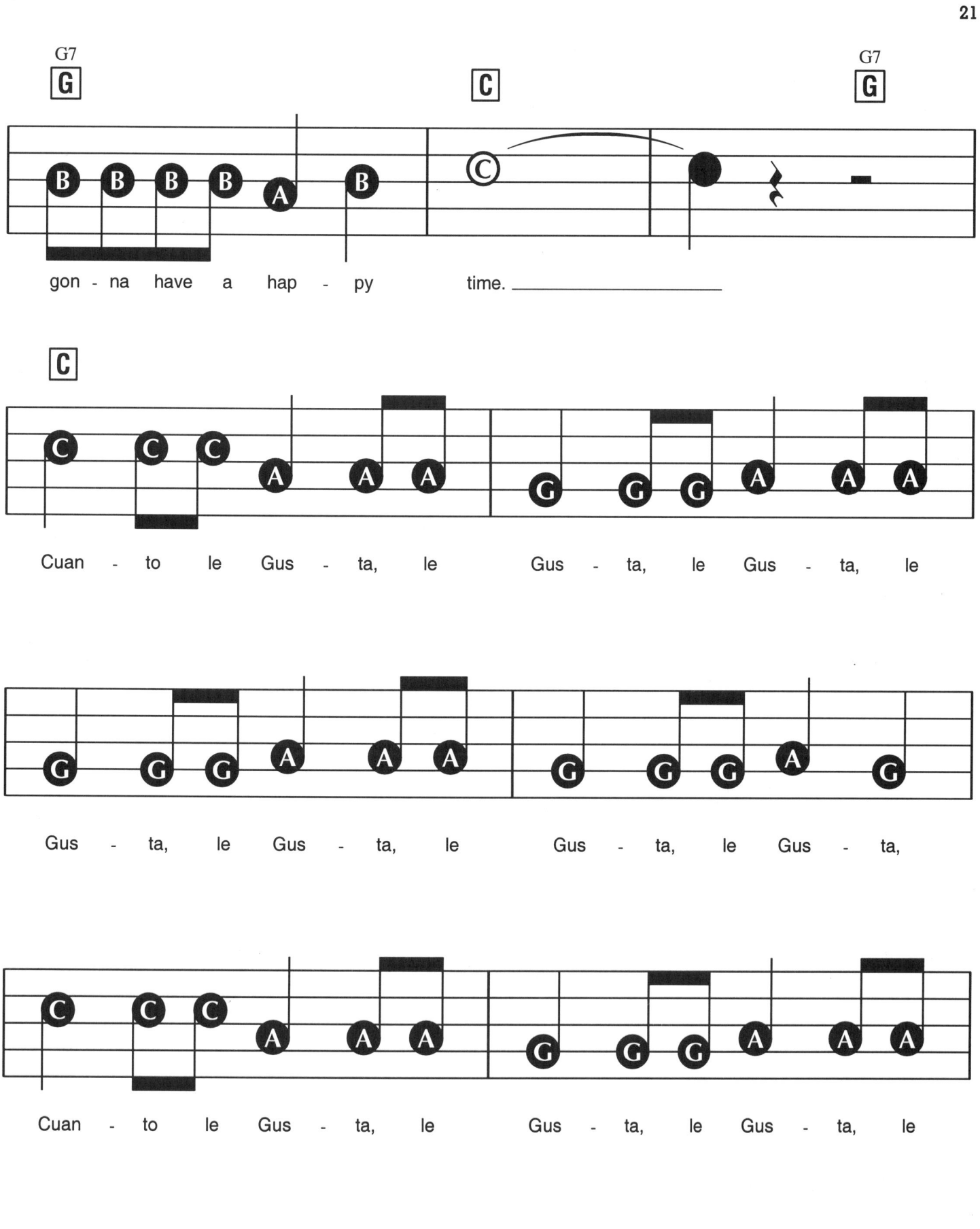

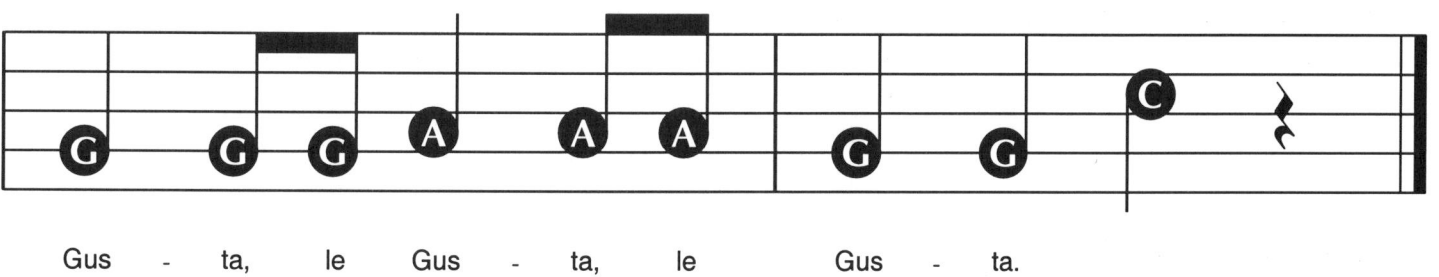

gon - na have a hap - py time. _____

Cuan - to le Gus - ta, le Gus - ta, le Gus - ta, le

Gus - ta, le Gus - ta, le Gus - ta, le Gus - ta,

Cuan - to le Gus - ta, le Gus - ta, le Gus - ta, le

Gus - ta, le Gus - ta, le Gus - ta.

Ciribiribin

Registration 7
Rhythm: Swing

Based on the original melody by A. Pestalozza
English Version by Harry James
and Jack Lawrence

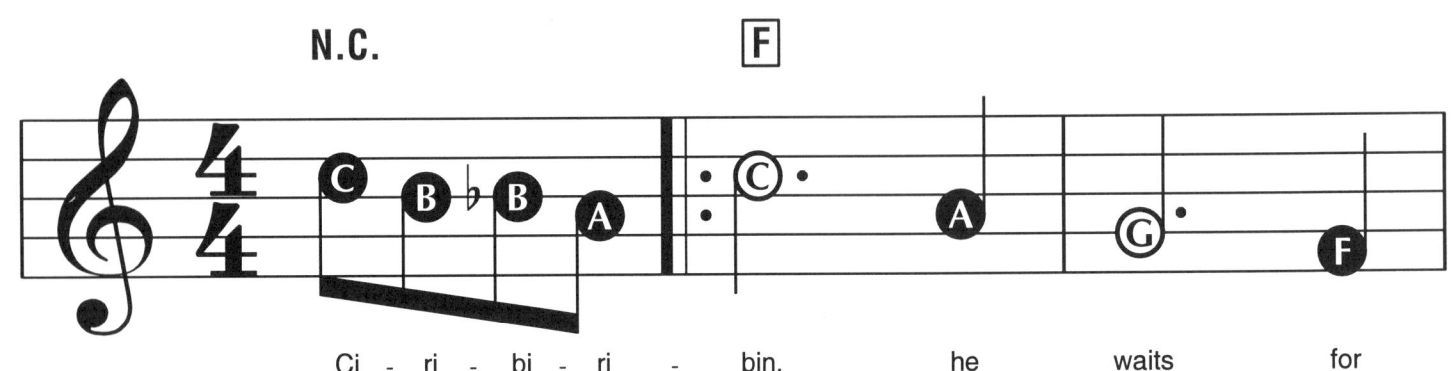
Ci - ri - bi - ri - bin, he waits for

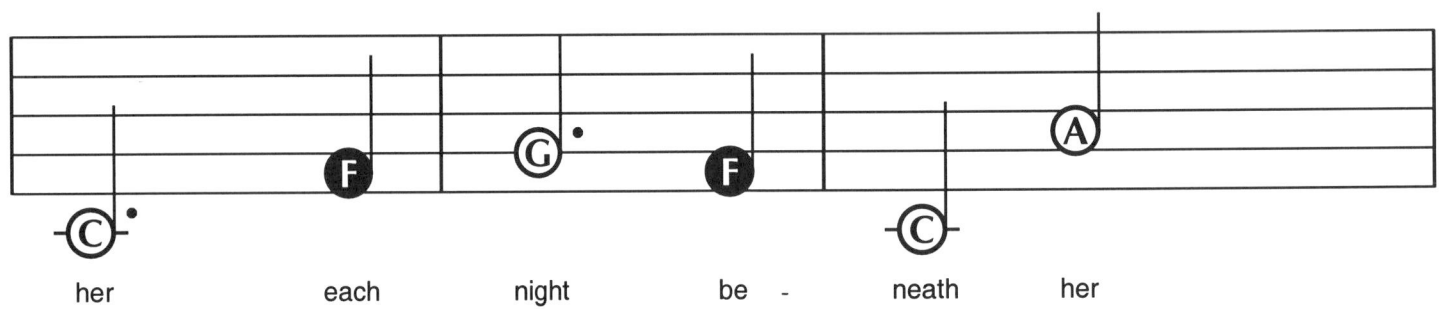
her each night be - neath her

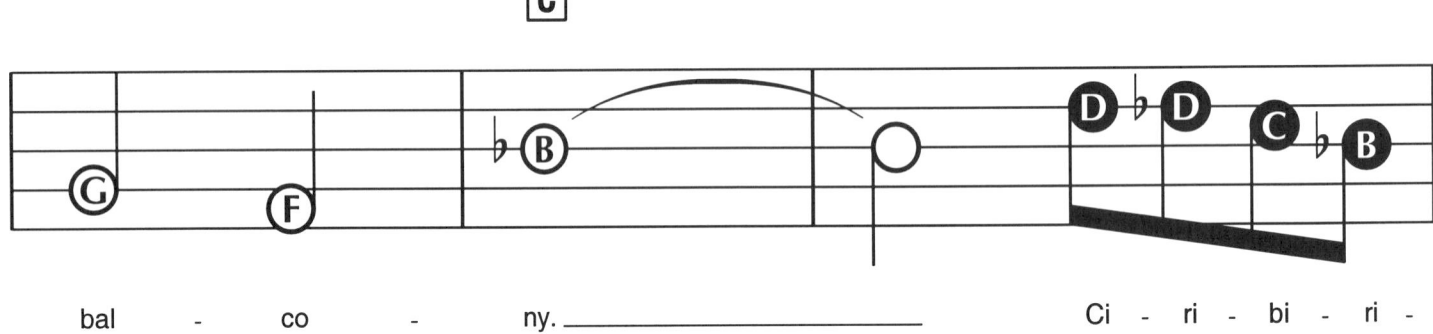
bal - co - ny. Ci - ri - bi - ri -

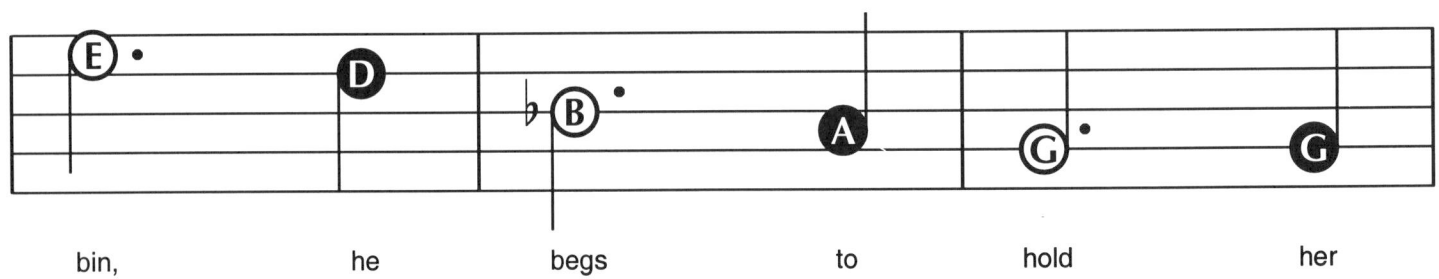
bin, he begs to hold her

Copyright © 1939 (Renewed 1966) and Assigned to Paramount Music Corporation
International Copyright Secured   All Rights Reserved

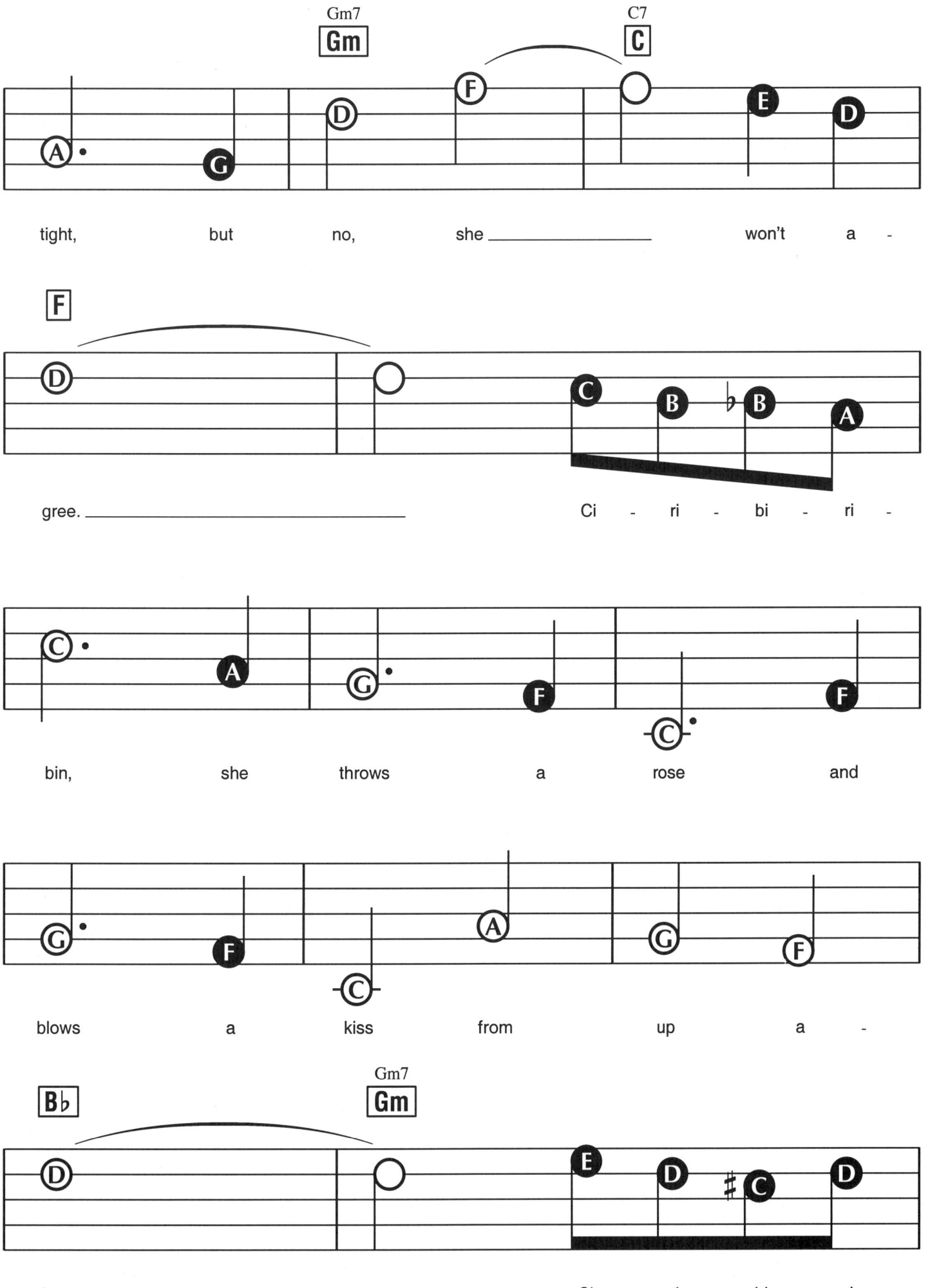

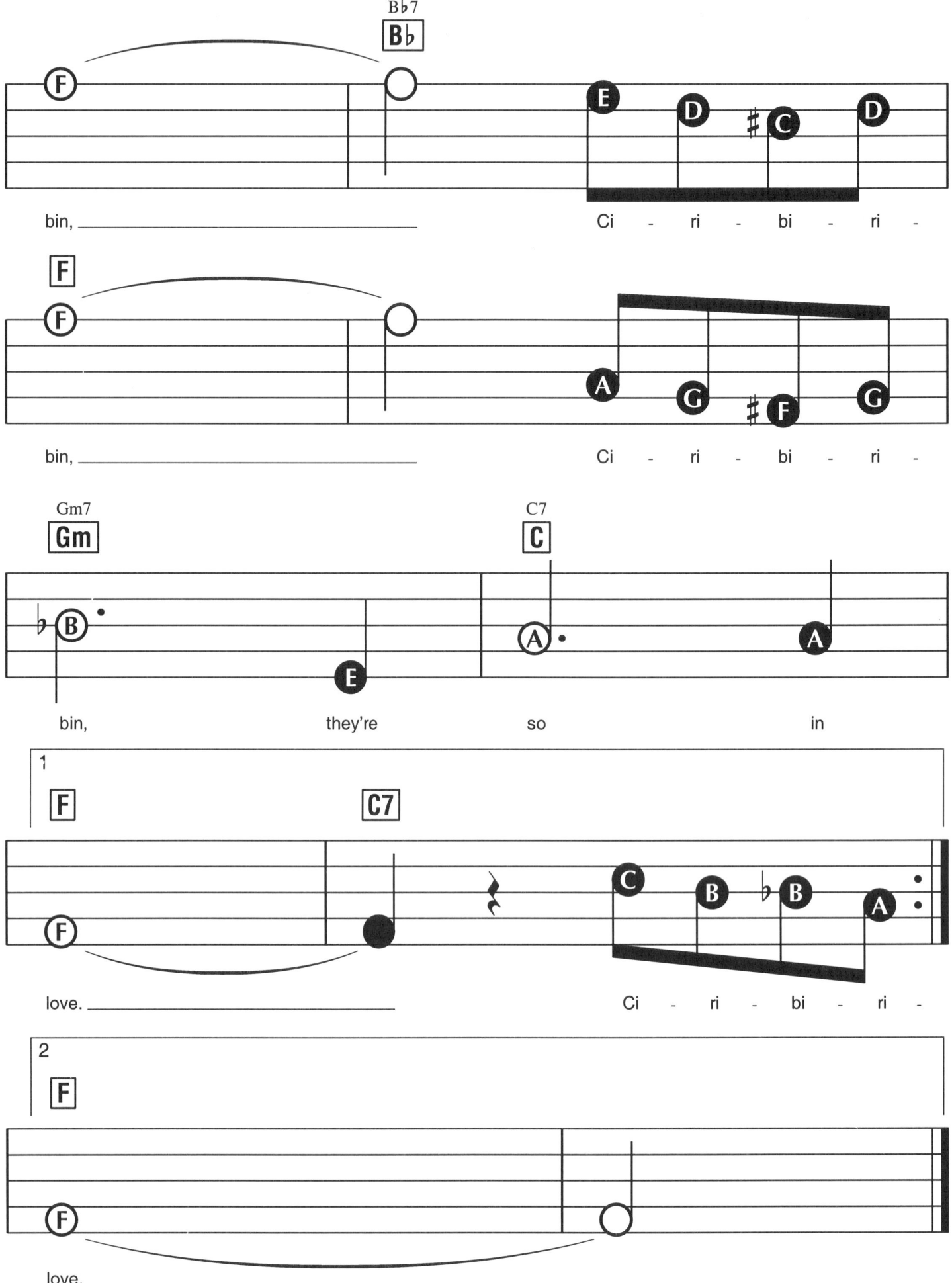

Dancing in the Street

Registration 5
Rhythm: Rock or 8 Beat

Words and Music by Marvin Gaye,
Ivy Hunter and William Stevenson

Call- ing out a- round the world are you
in- vi- ta- tion across the world na- tion a

rea- dy for a brand new beat
chance for folks to meet there'll

sum- mer's here and the time is right for
be laugh- ing sing- ing and mu- sic swinging

danc- ing in the street. They're danc- ing in Chi-
danc- ing in the street. Phila- del- phia, P. A.,

ca- go, down in New Or- leans,
Baltimore and D. C. Now

© 1964 (Renewed 1992) FCG MUSIC, NMG MUSIC, MGIII MUSIC, JOBETE MUSIC CO., INC. and STONE AGATE MUSIC
All Rights Controlled and Administered by EMI APRIL MUSIC INC. and EMI BLACKWOOD MUSIC INC
on behalf of JOBETE MUSIC CO., INC. and STONE AGATE MUSIC (A Division of JOBETE MUSIC CO., INC.)
All Rights Reserved   International Copyright Secured   Used by Permission

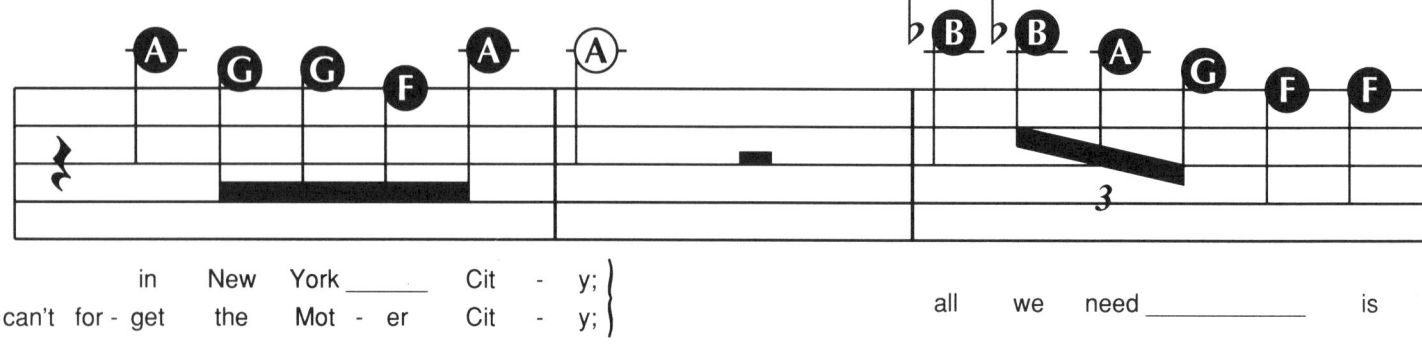
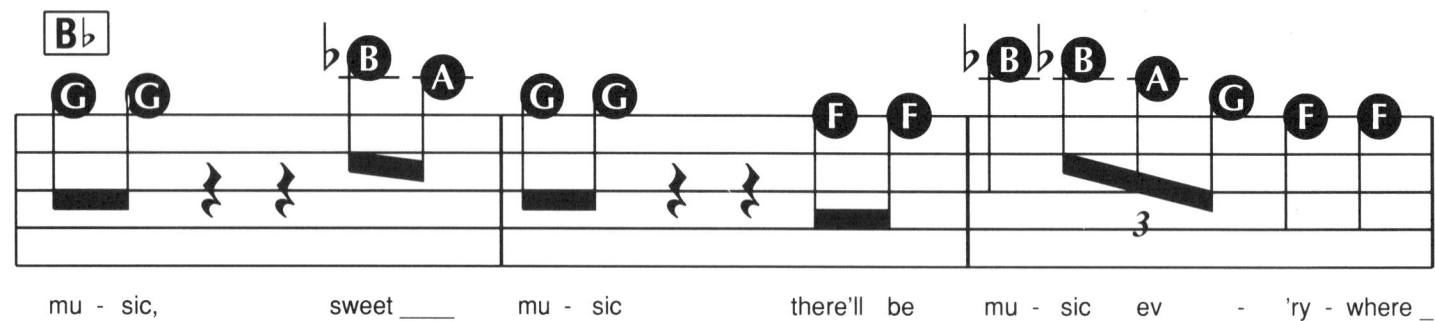
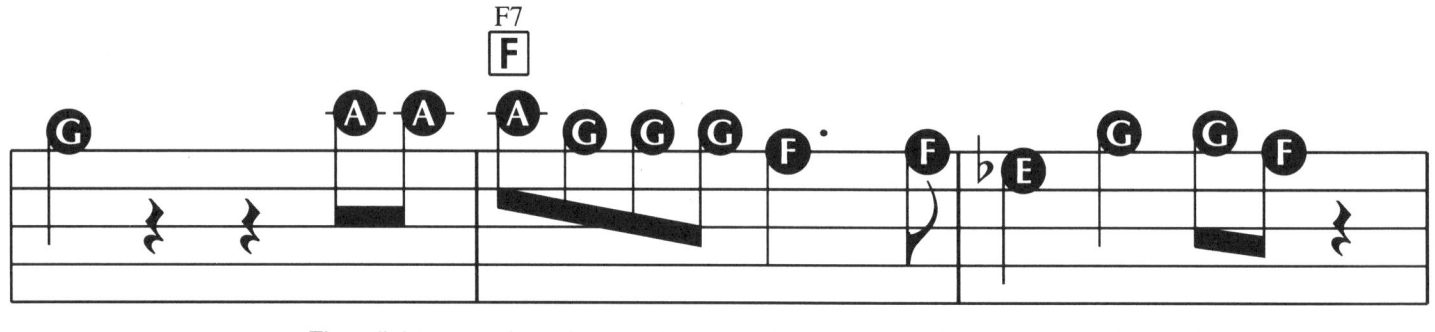
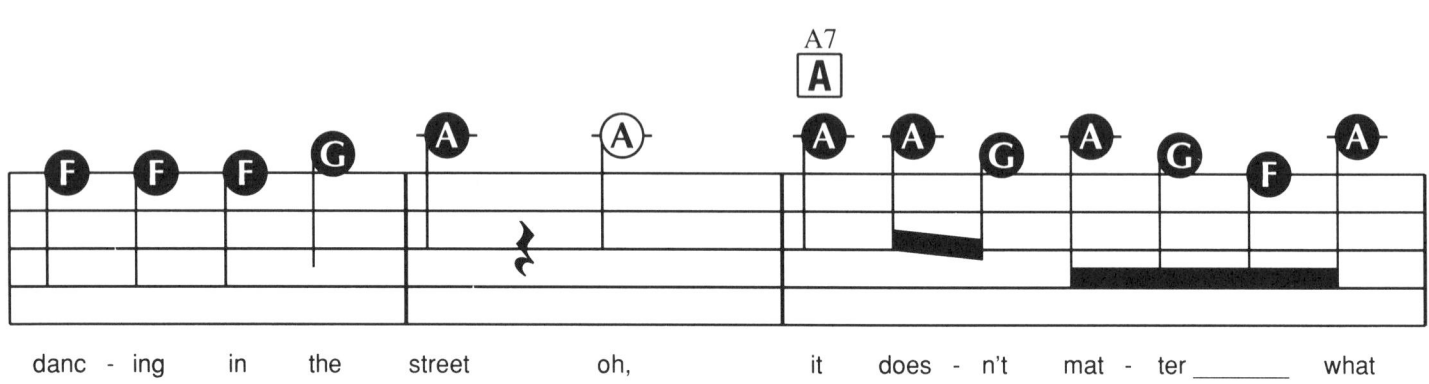
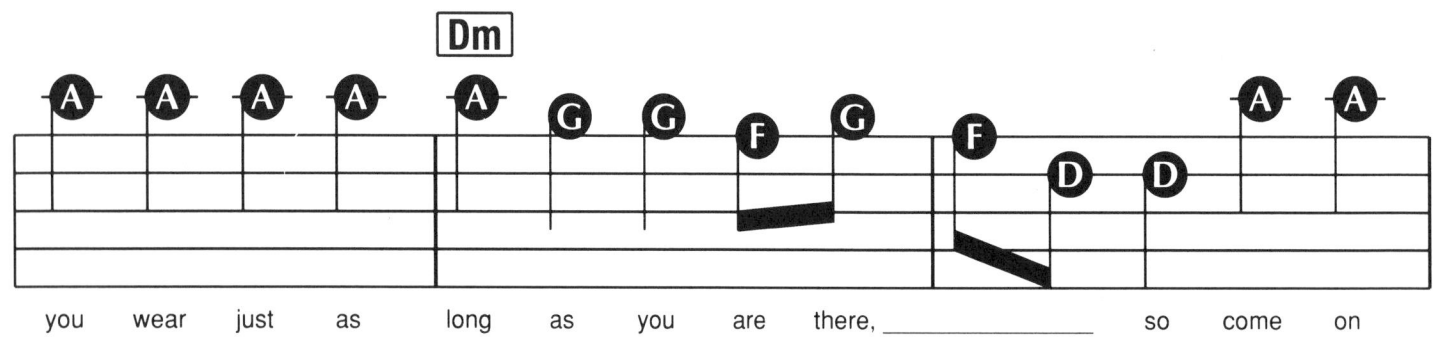

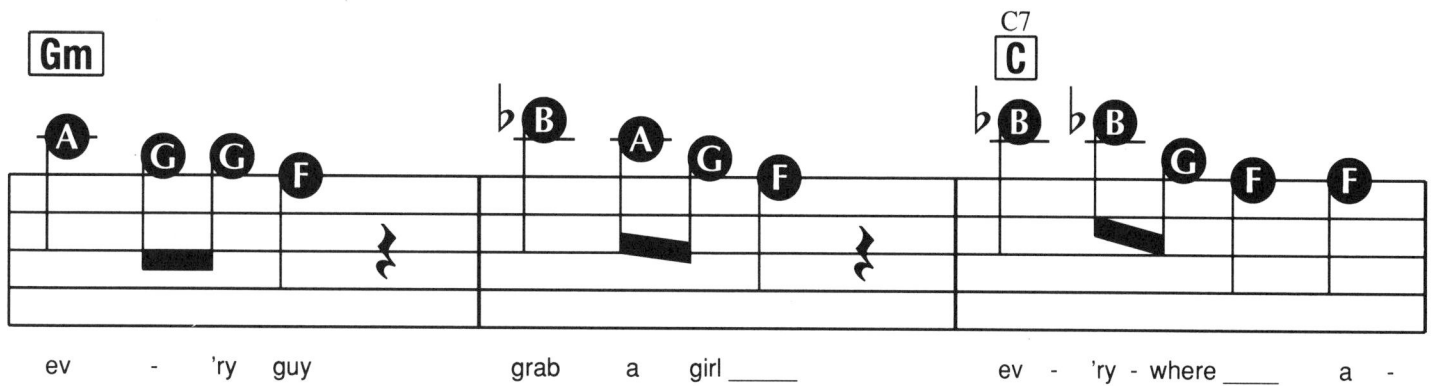
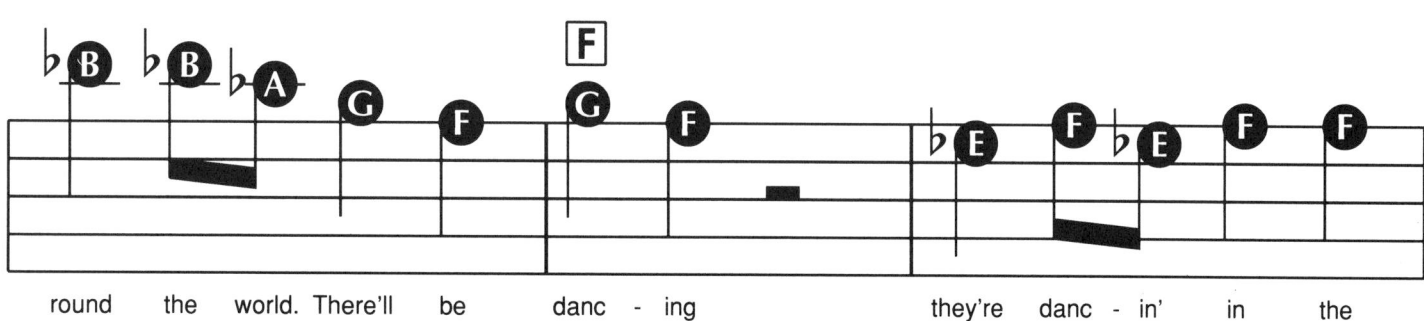
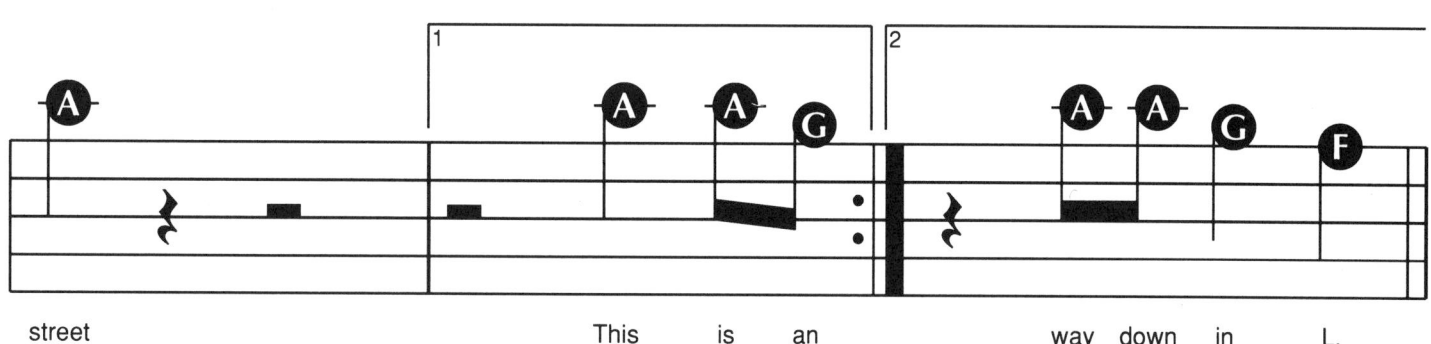
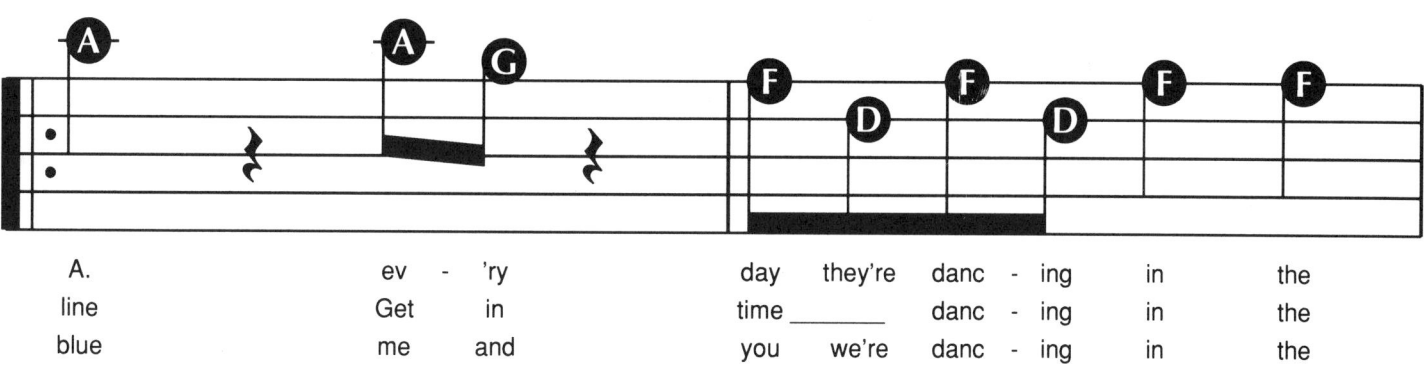
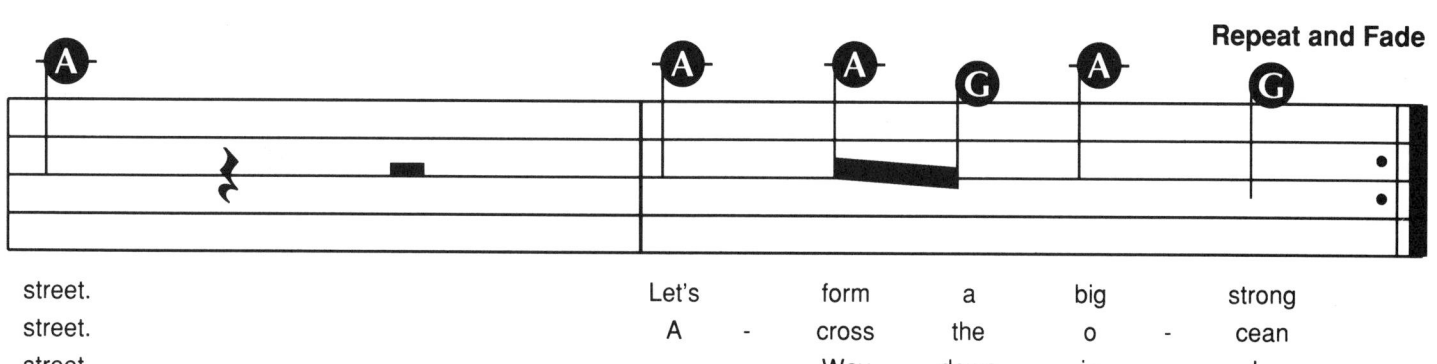

Fly Me to the Moon
(In Other Words)
featured in the Motion Picture ONCE AROUND

Registration 2
Rhythm: Waltz or Jazz Waltz

Words and Music by
Bart Howard

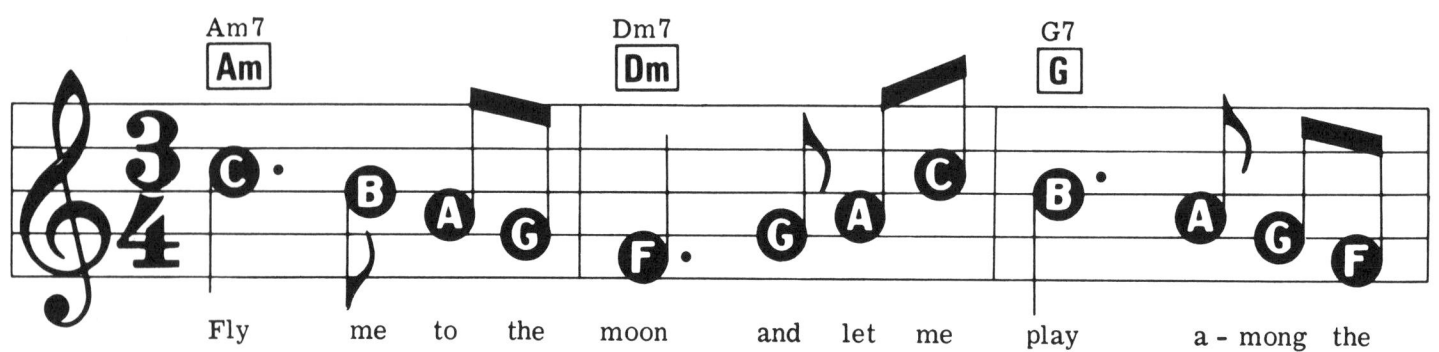

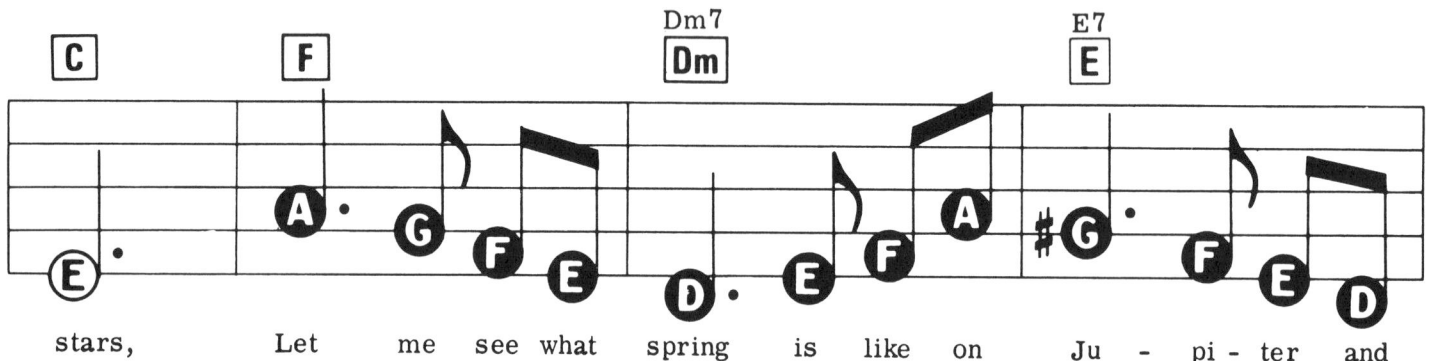

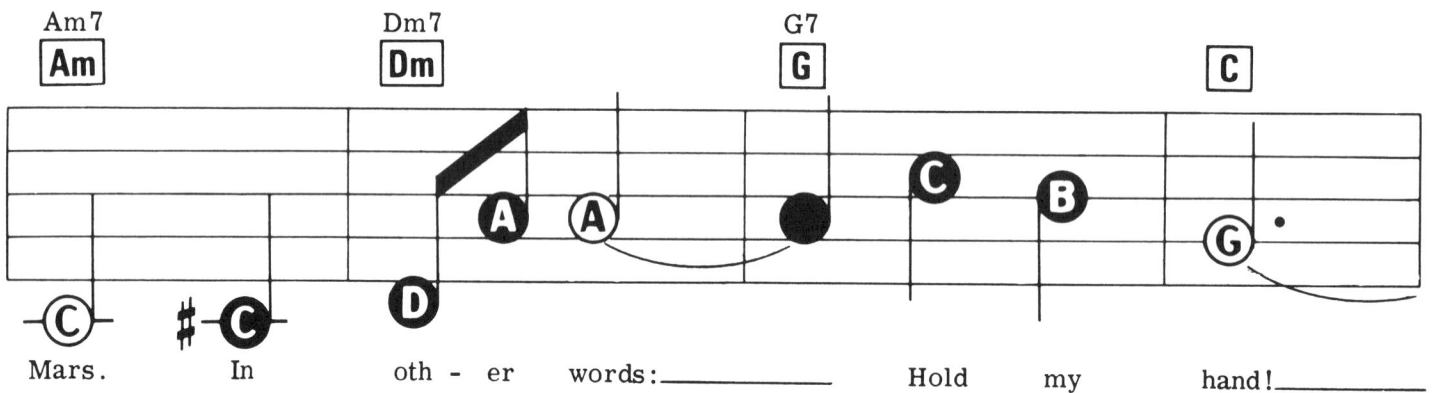

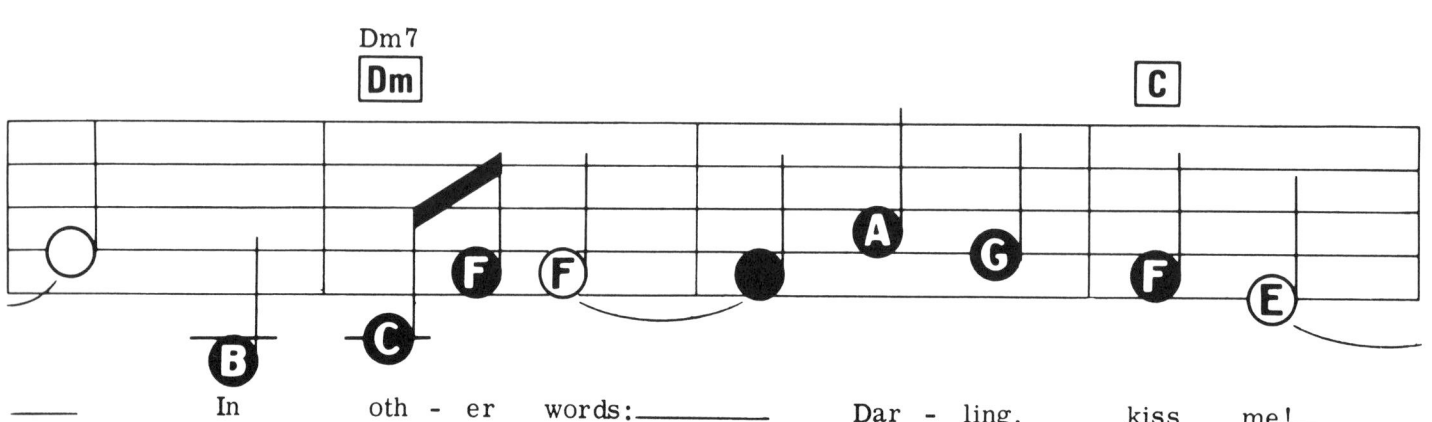

TRO - © Copyright 1954 (Renewed) Hampshire House Publishing Corp., New York, NY
International Copyright Secured
All Rights Reserved Including Public Performance For Profit
Used by Permission

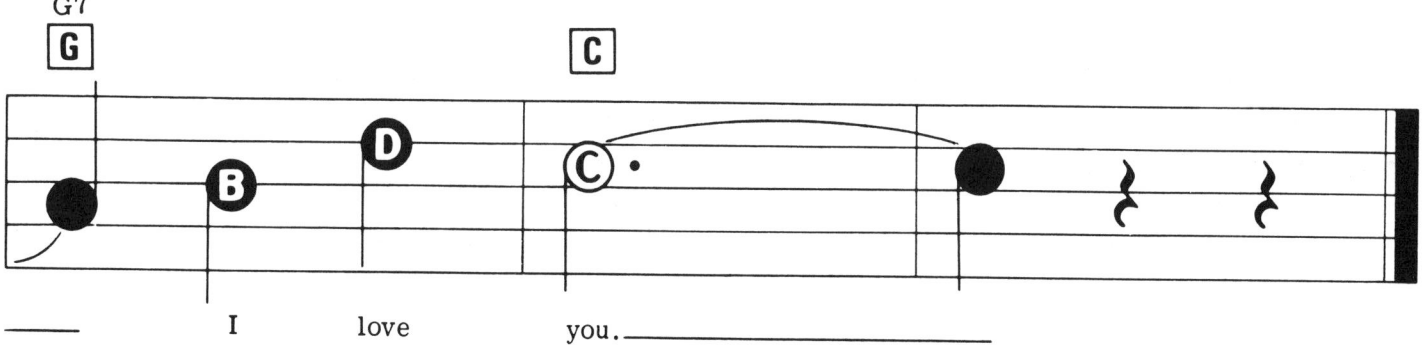

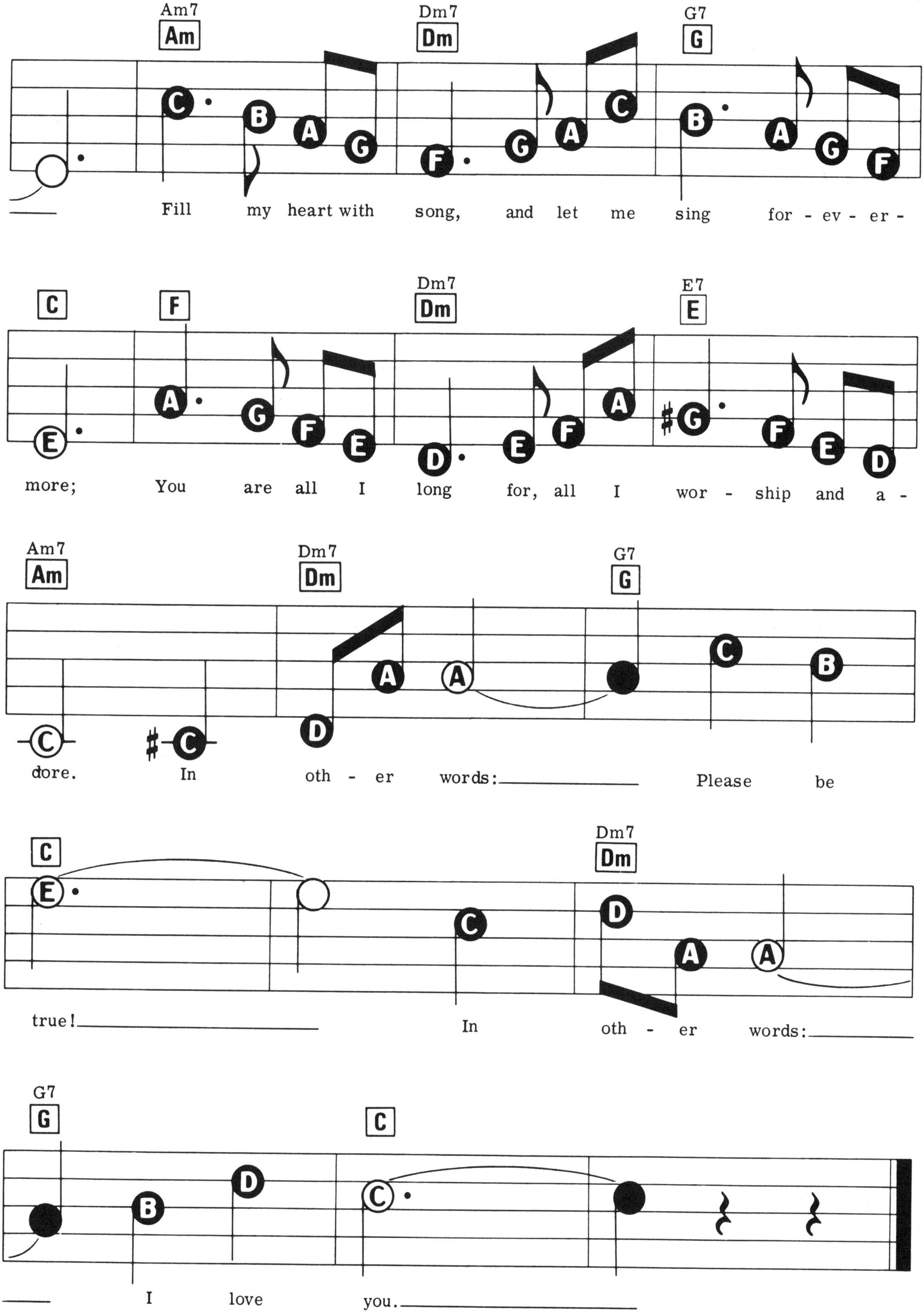

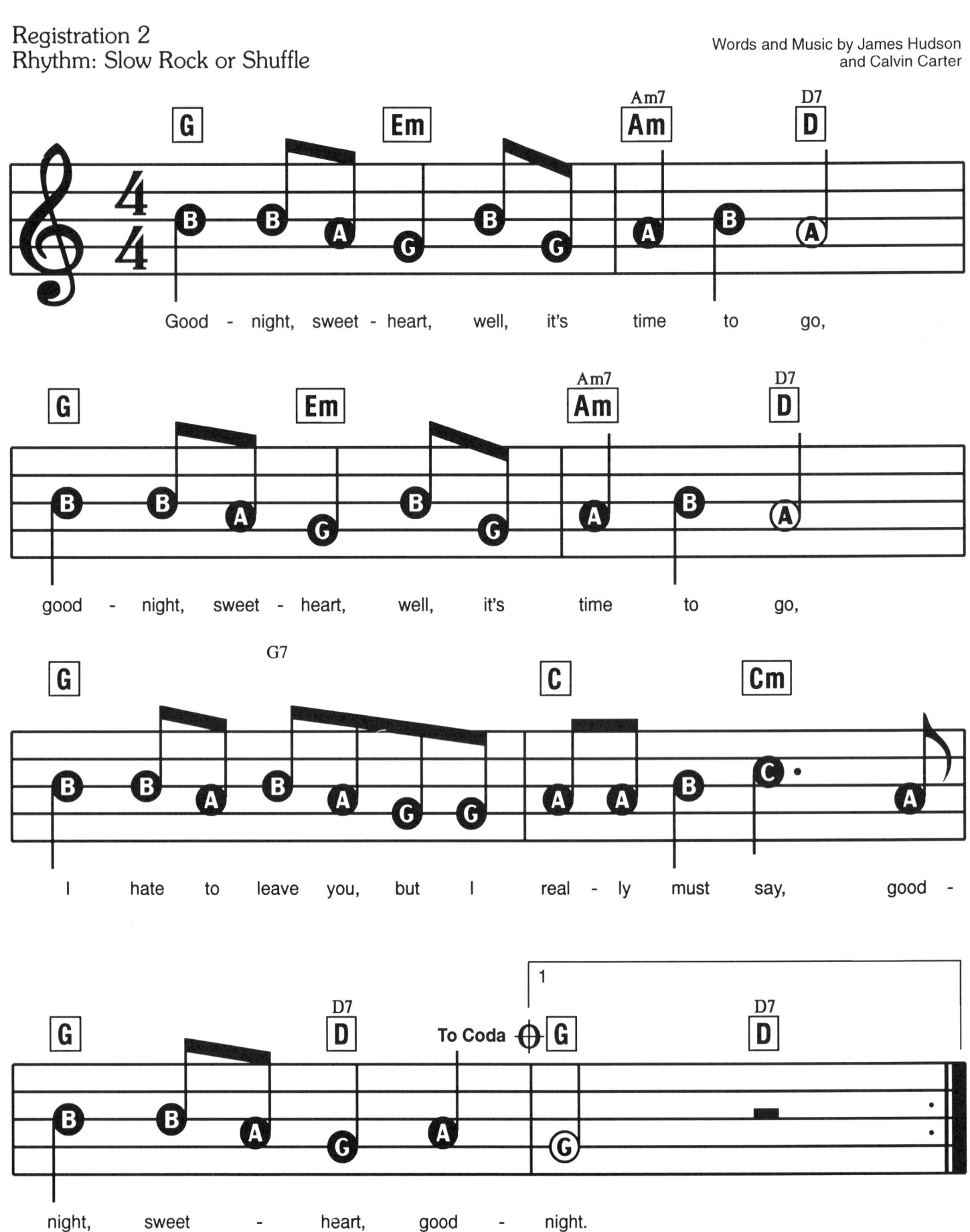

The Great Pretender

Registration 4
Rhythm: Fox Trot or Swing

Words and Music by
Buck Ram

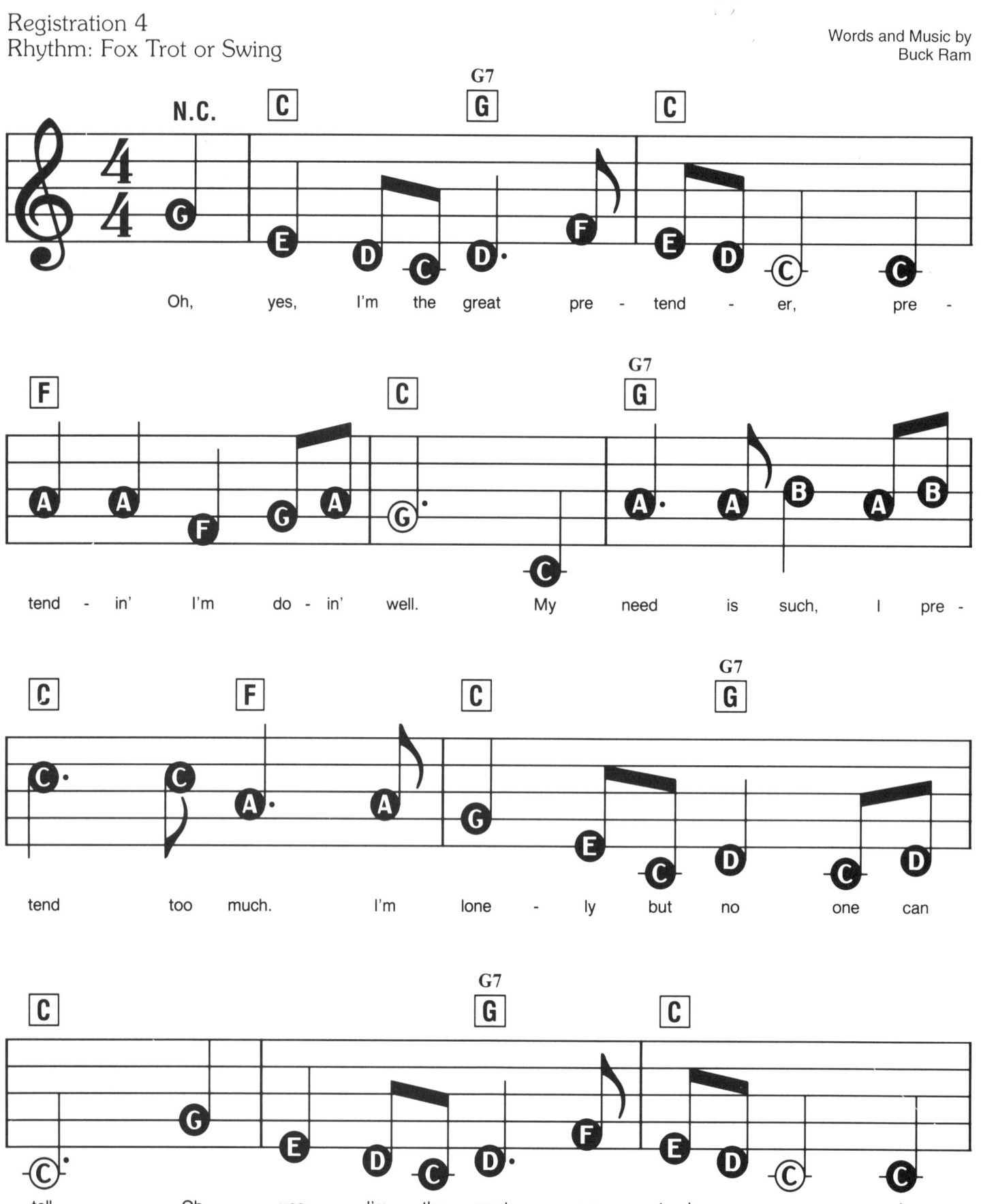

Copyright © 1955 by Panther Music Corp.
Copyright Renewed
International Copyright Secured   All Rights Reserved

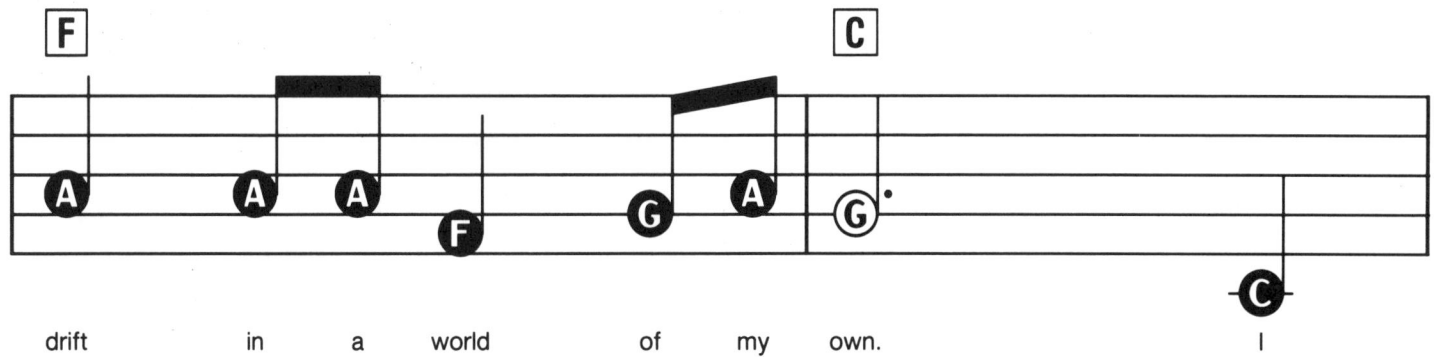
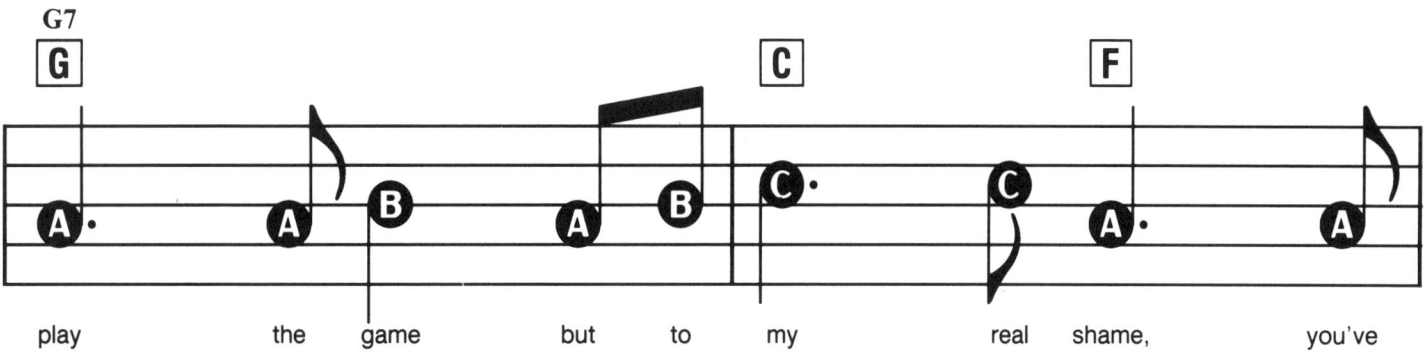
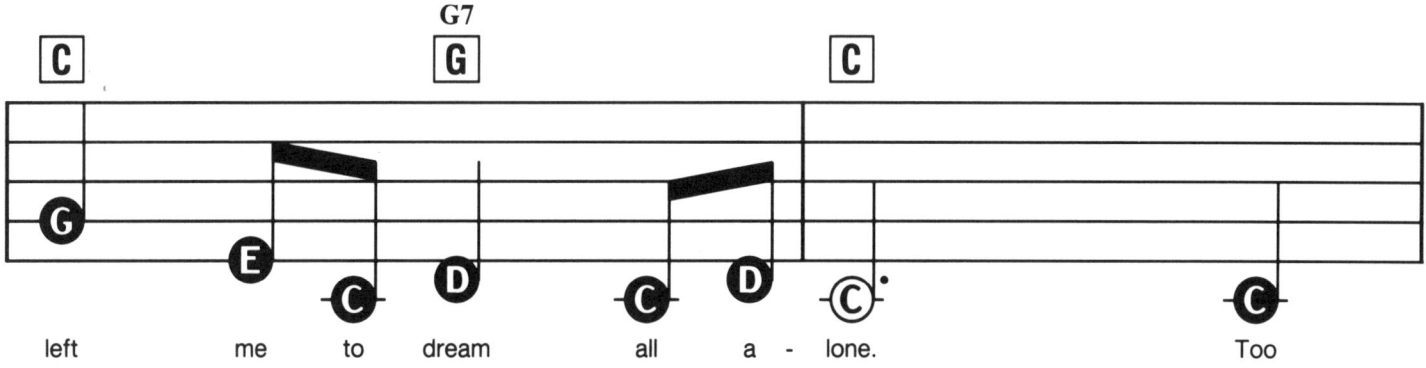
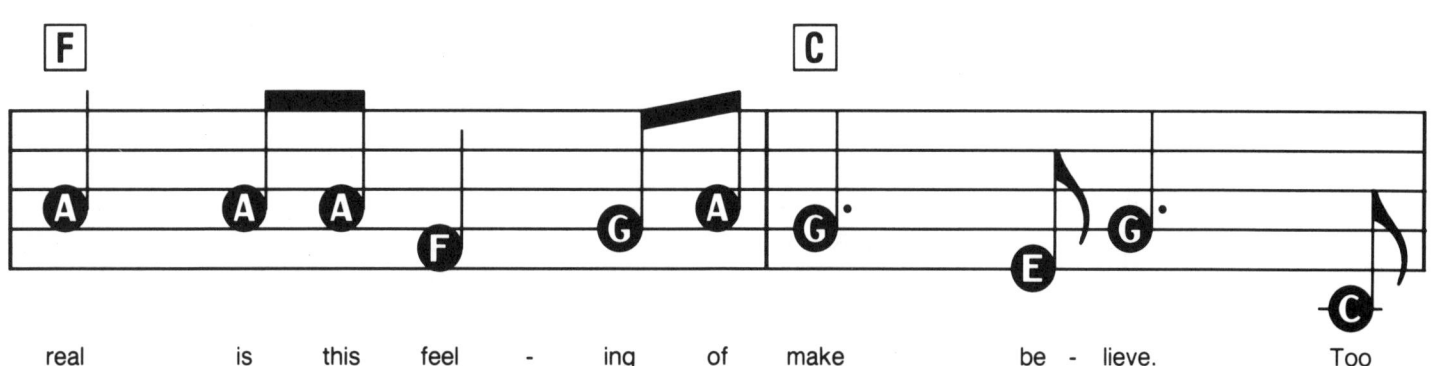

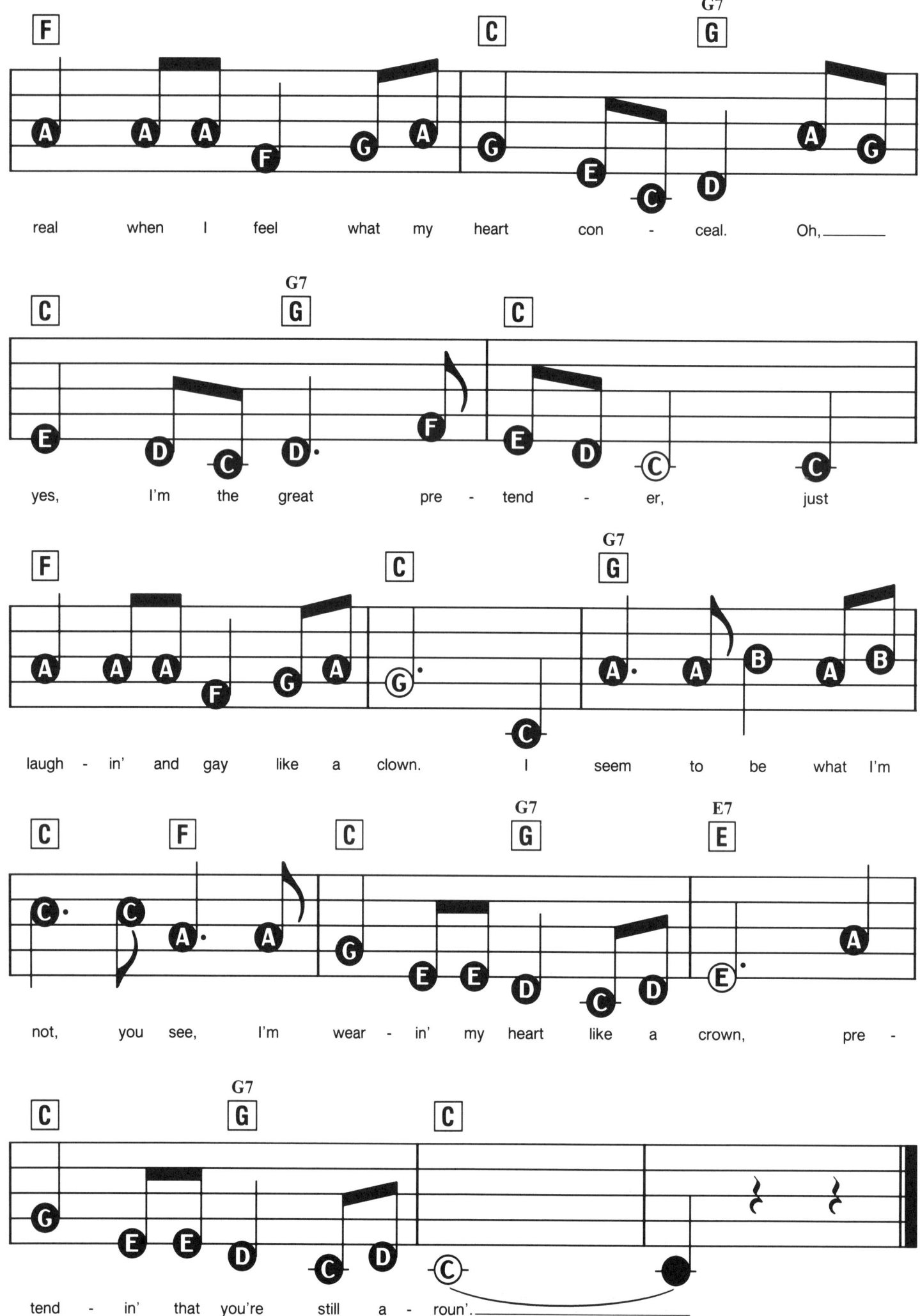

In the Mood

Registration 8
Rhythm: Swing

By Joe Garland

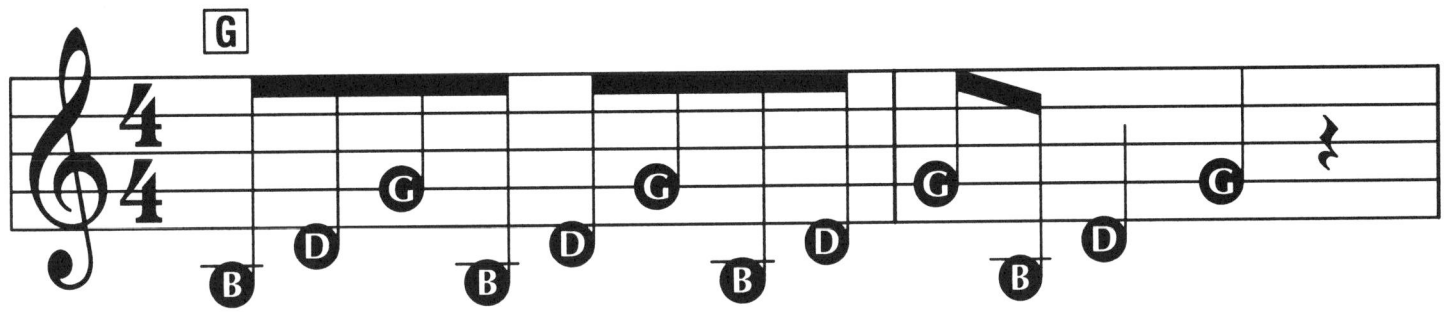

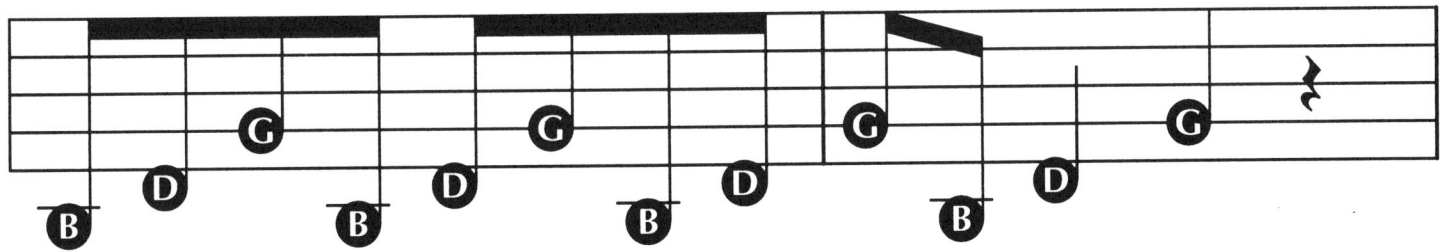

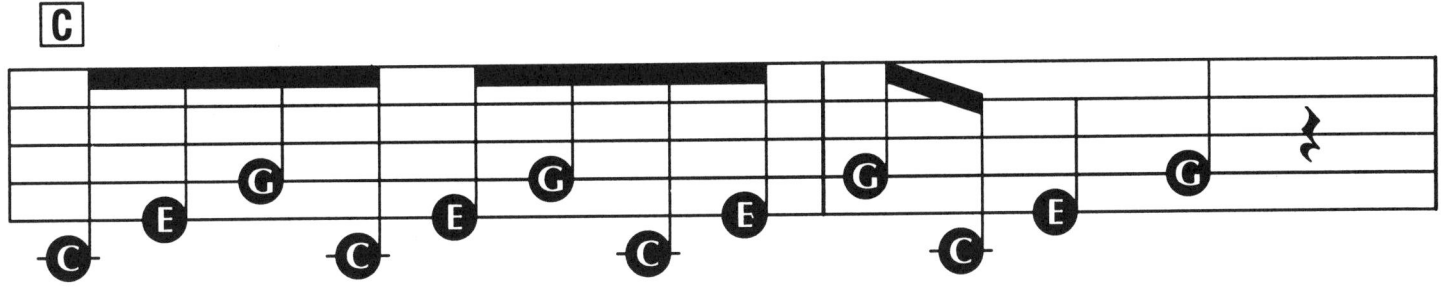

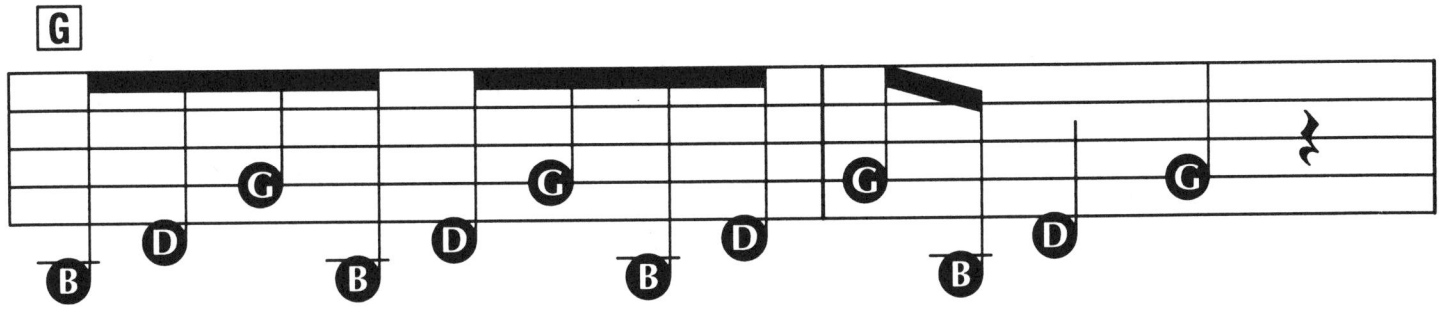

Copyright © 1939, 1960 Shapiro, Bernstein & Co., Inc., New York
Copyright Renewed
International Copyright Secured   All Rights Reserved
Used by Permission

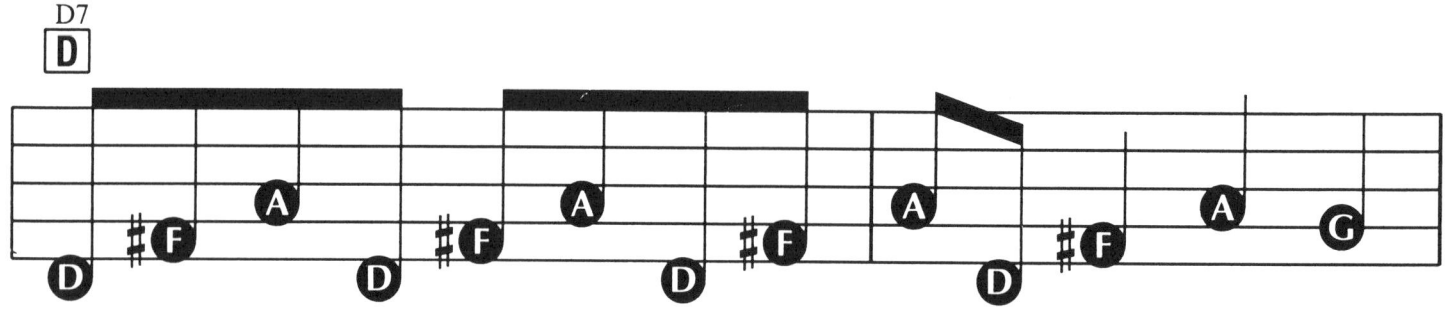
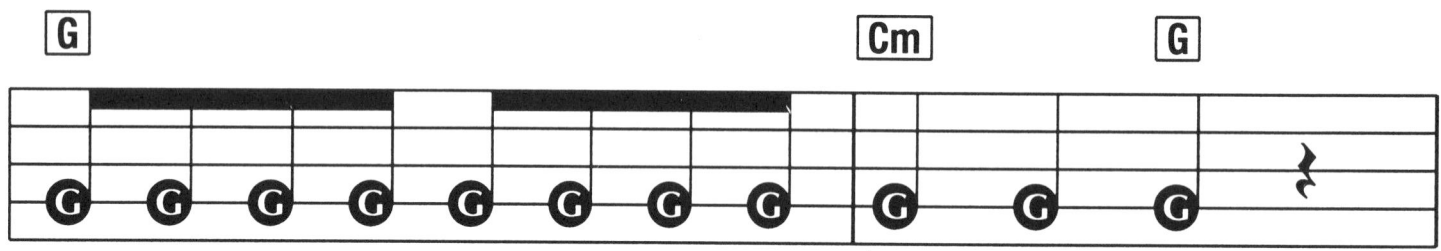
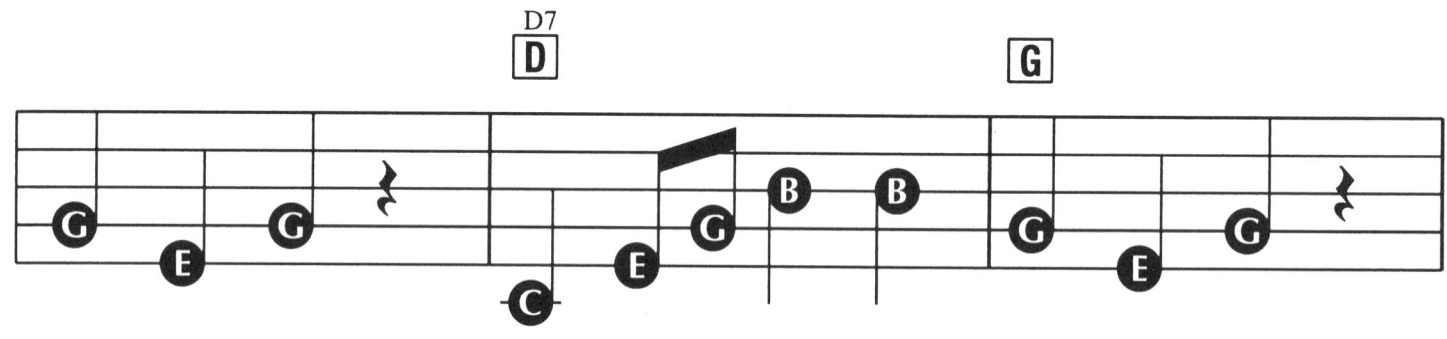
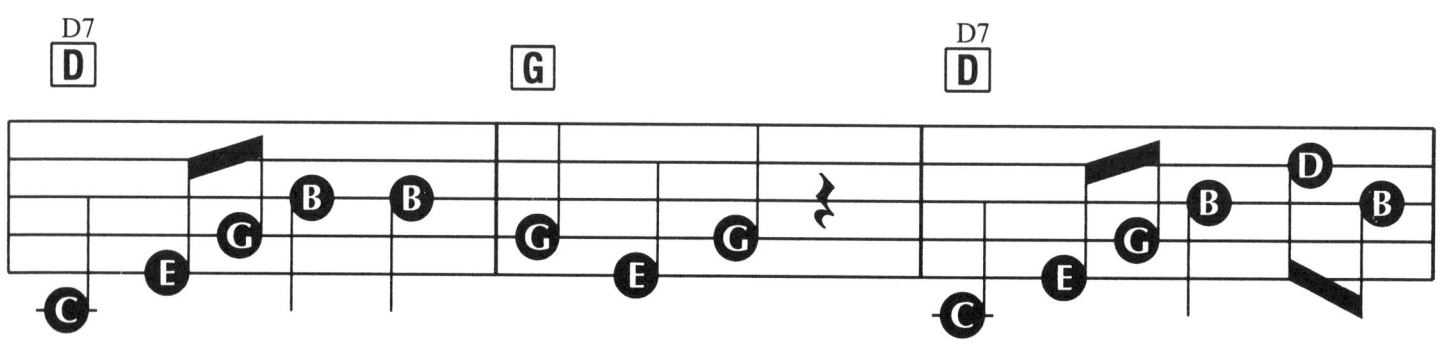

37

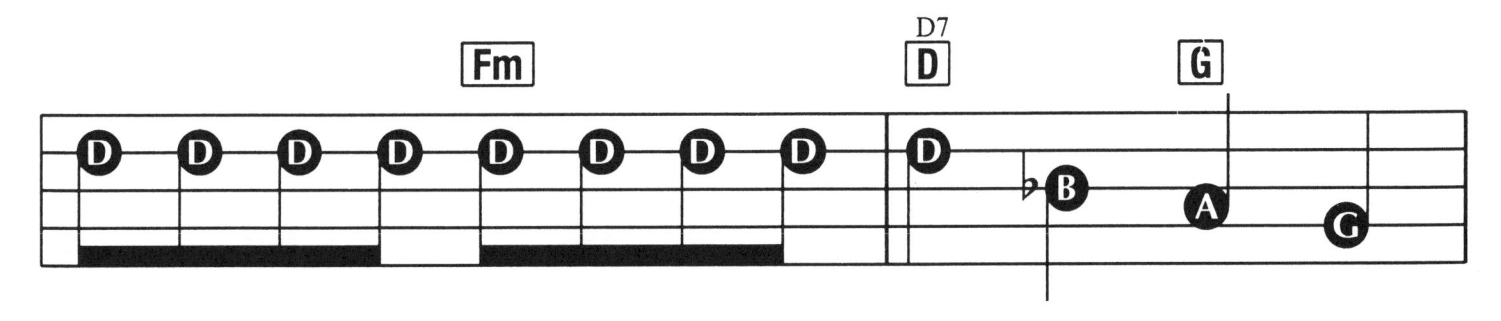

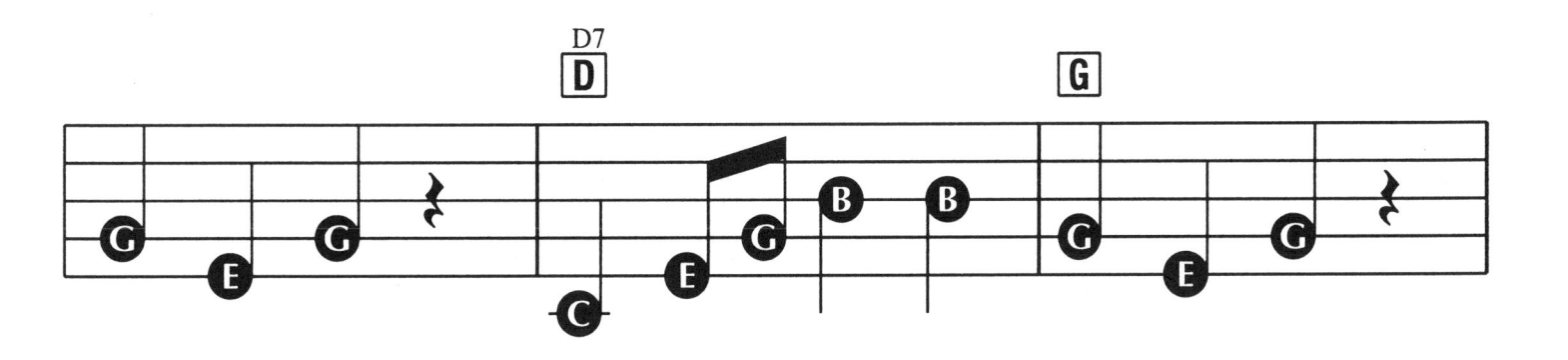

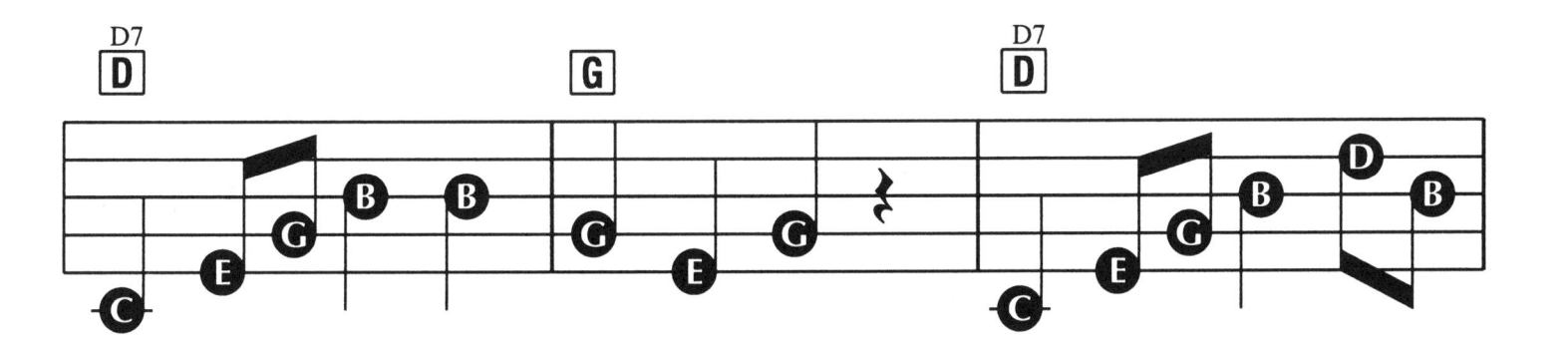

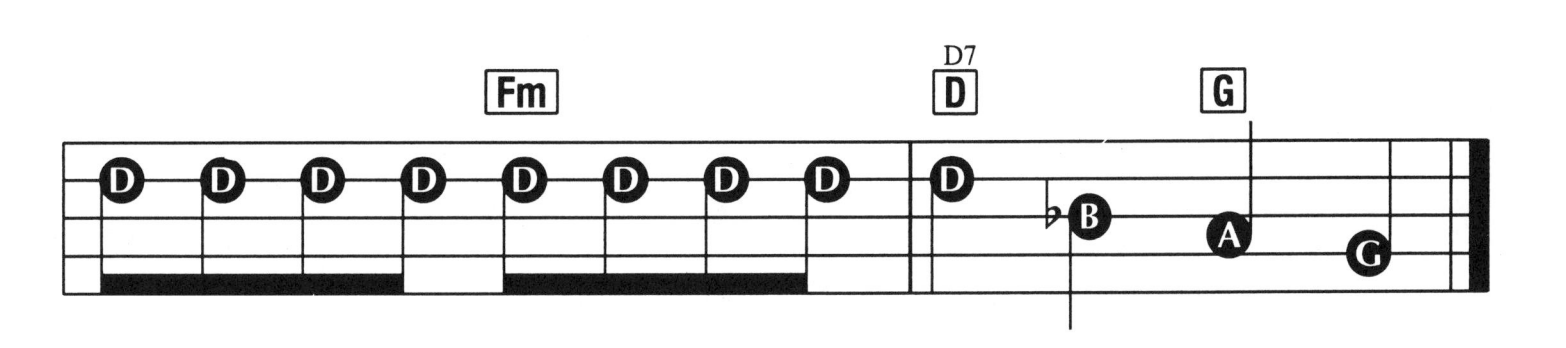

The Loco-Motion

Registration 4
Rhythm: Rock

Words and Music by Gerry Goffin
and Carole King

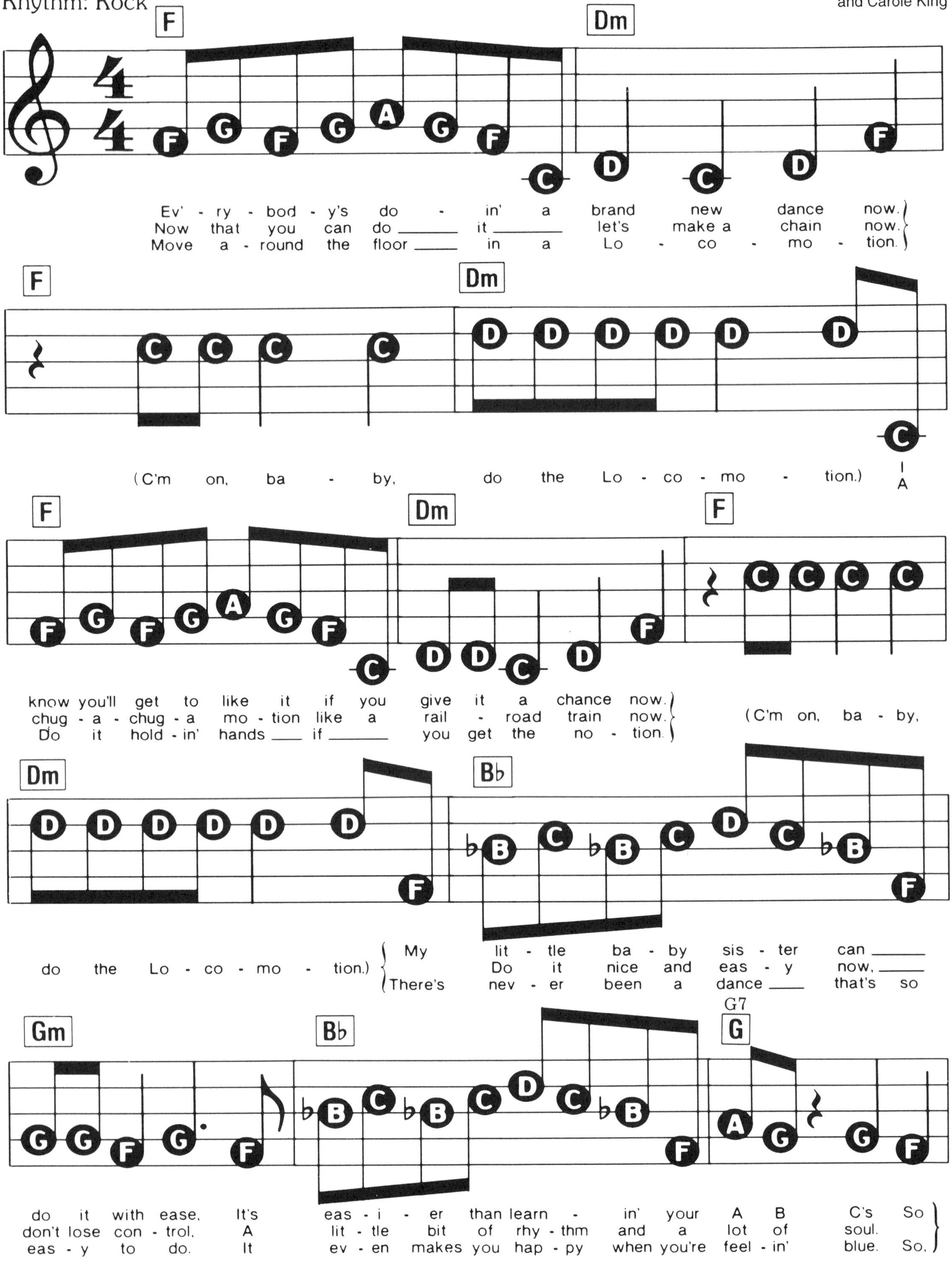

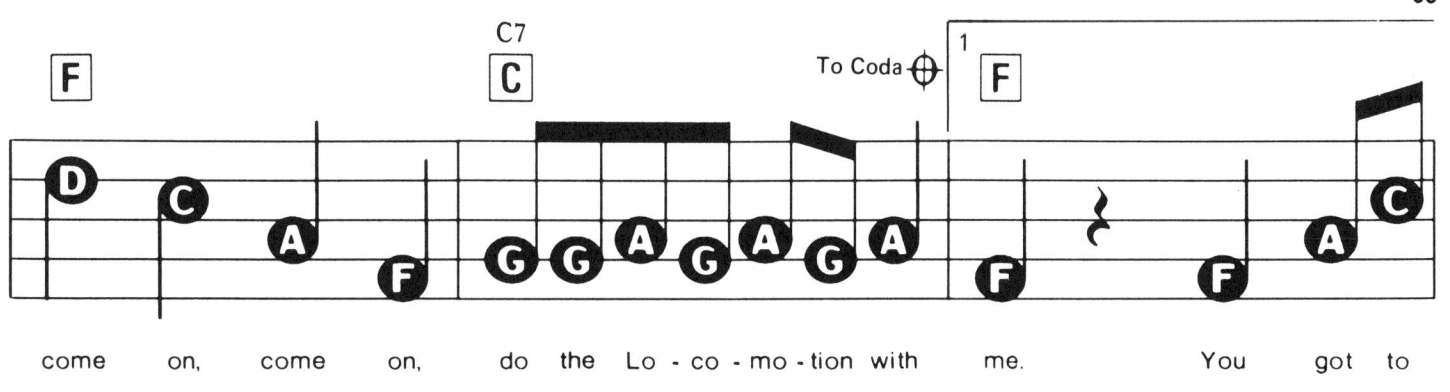

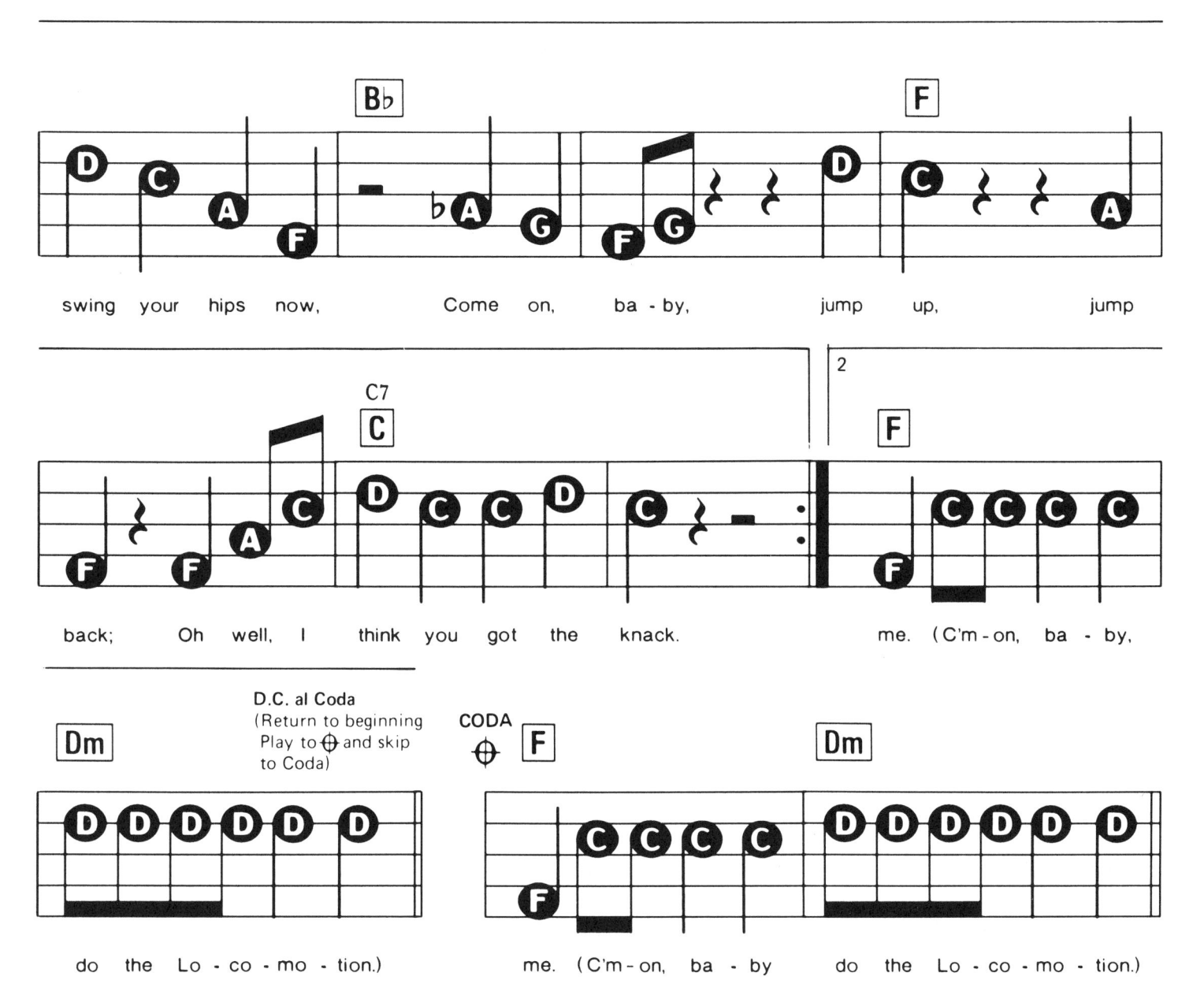

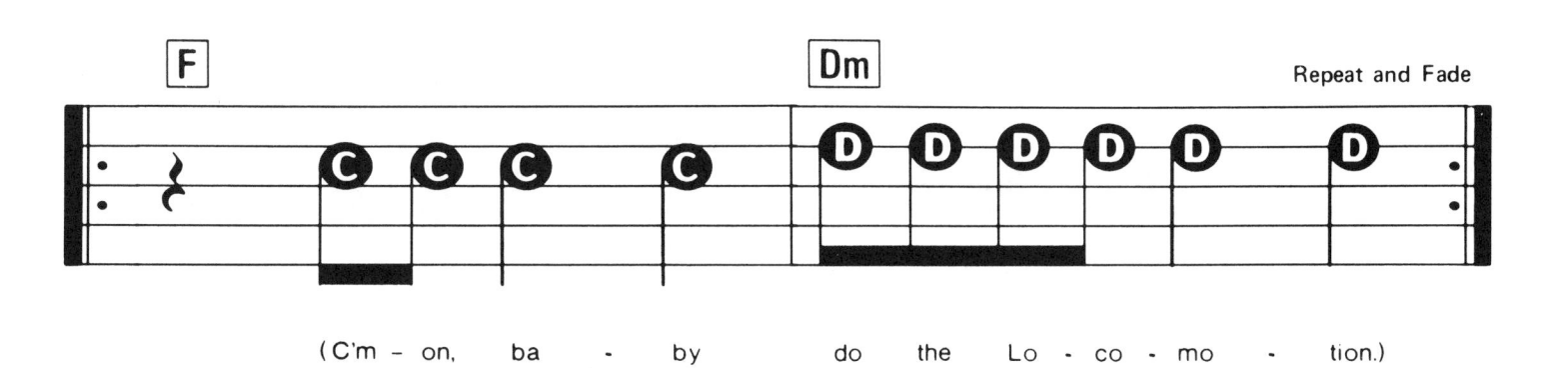

come on, come on, do the Lo-co-mo-tion with me. You got to swing your hips now, Come on, ba-by, jump up, jump back; Oh well, I think you got the knack. me. (C'm-on, ba-by, do the Lo-co-mo-tion.) me. (C'm-on, ba-by do the Lo-co-mo-tion.) (C'm-on, ba-by do the Lo-co-mo-tion.)

The Look of Love
from CASINO ROYALE

Registration 4
Rhythm: Bossa Nova

Words by Hal David
Music by Burt Bacharach

The look of love is in your eyes; a look your smile can't dis-guise.
The look of love; it's on your face, a look that time can't e-rase.

The look of love; it's say-ing so much more than just words could ev-er say. And what my heart has heard, well, it takes my breath a-way.
Be mine to-night. Let this be just the start of so man-y nights like this. Let's take a lov-er's vow, and then seal it with a kiss.

© 1967 (Renewed 1995) COLGEMS-EMI MUSIC INC.
All Rights Reserved International Copyright Secured Used by Permission

41

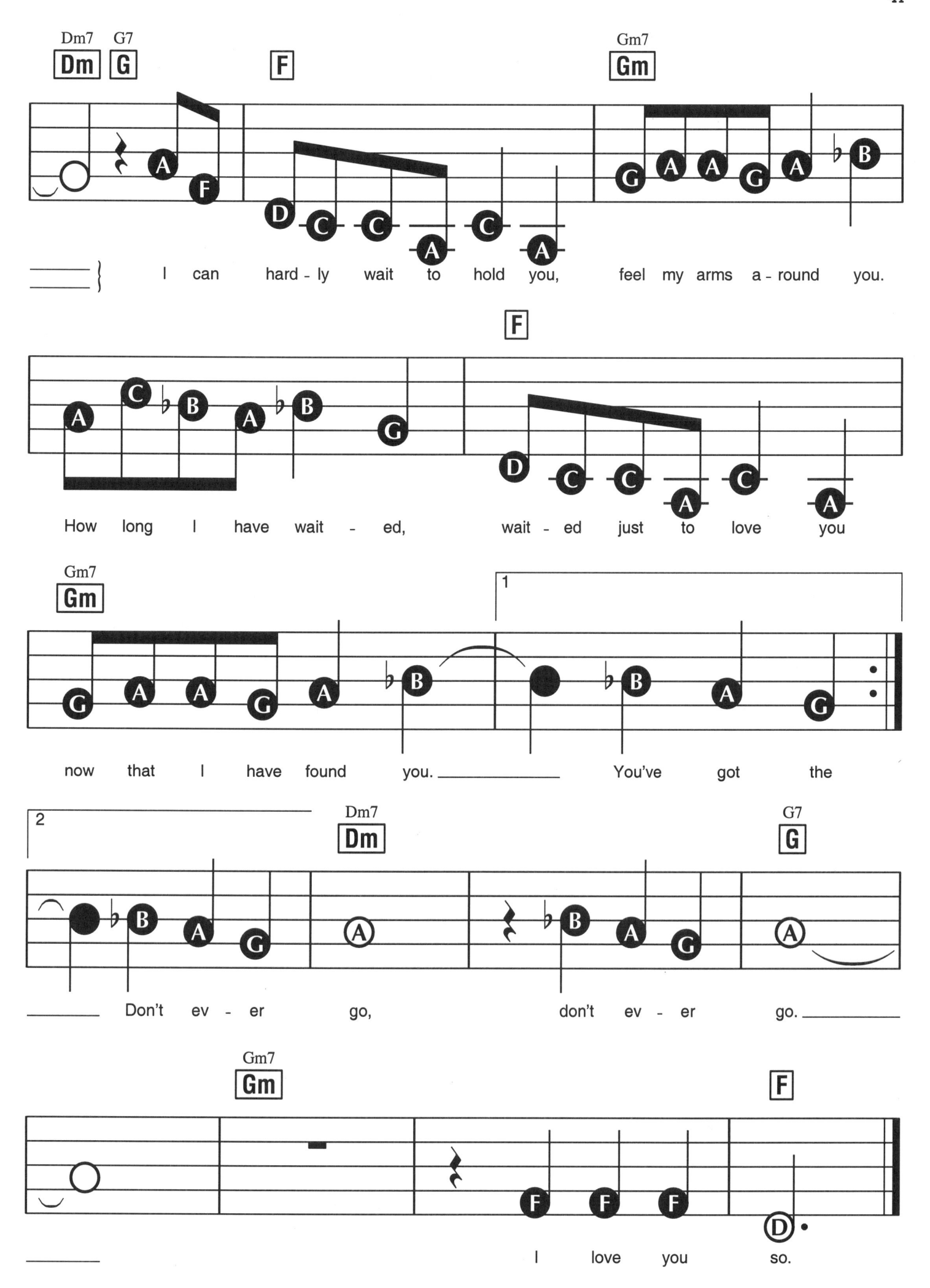

I can hard-ly wait to hold you, feel my arms a-round you.

How long I have wait-ed, wait-ed just to love you

now that I have found you. You've got the

Don't ev-er go, don't ev-er go.

I love you so.

42

L-O-V-E

Registration 8
Rhythm: Fox Trot or Swing

Words and Music by Bert Kaempfert
and Milt Gabler

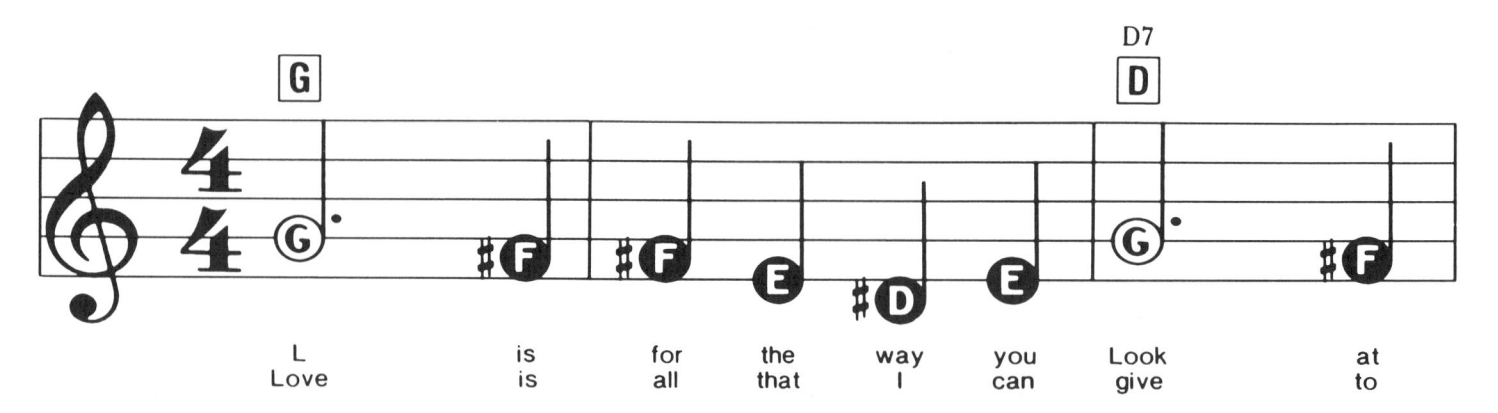

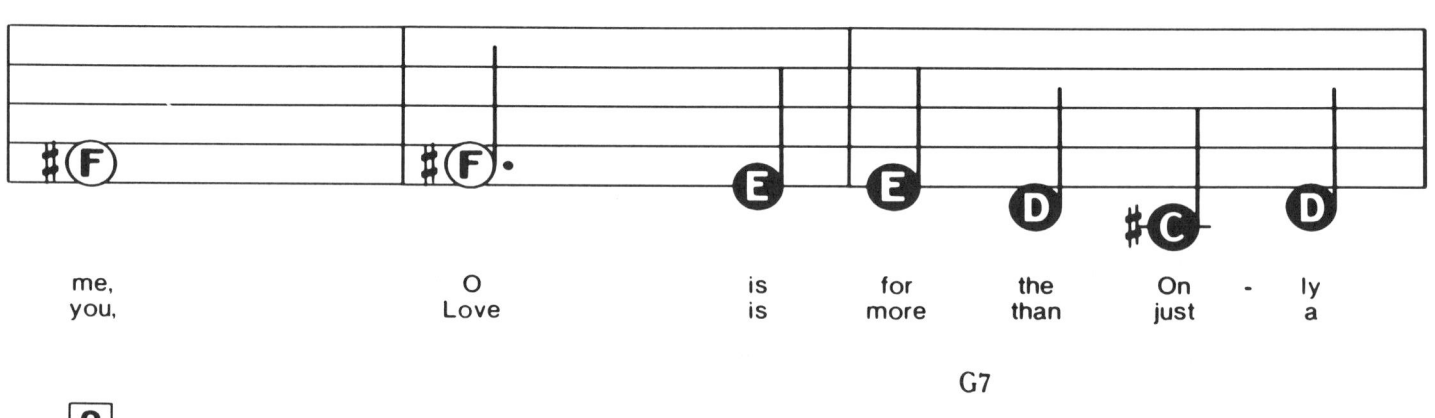

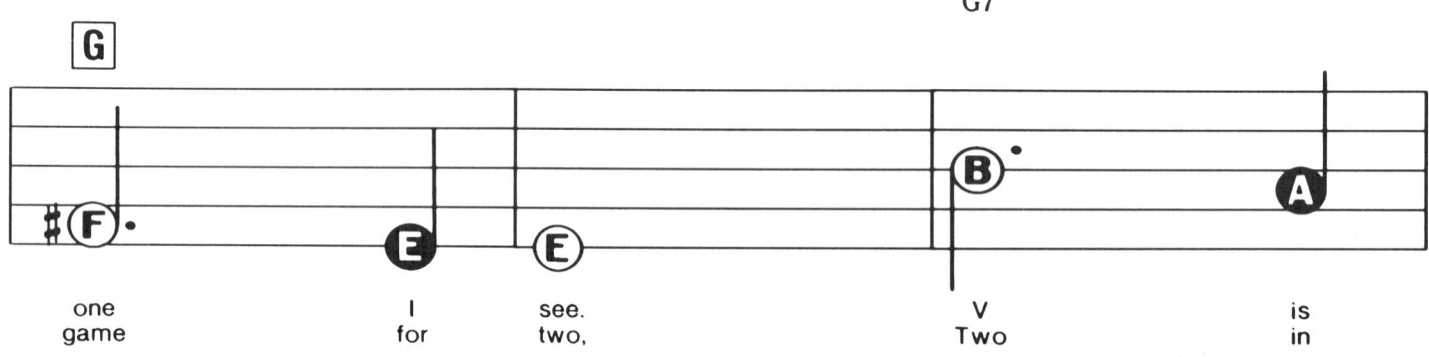

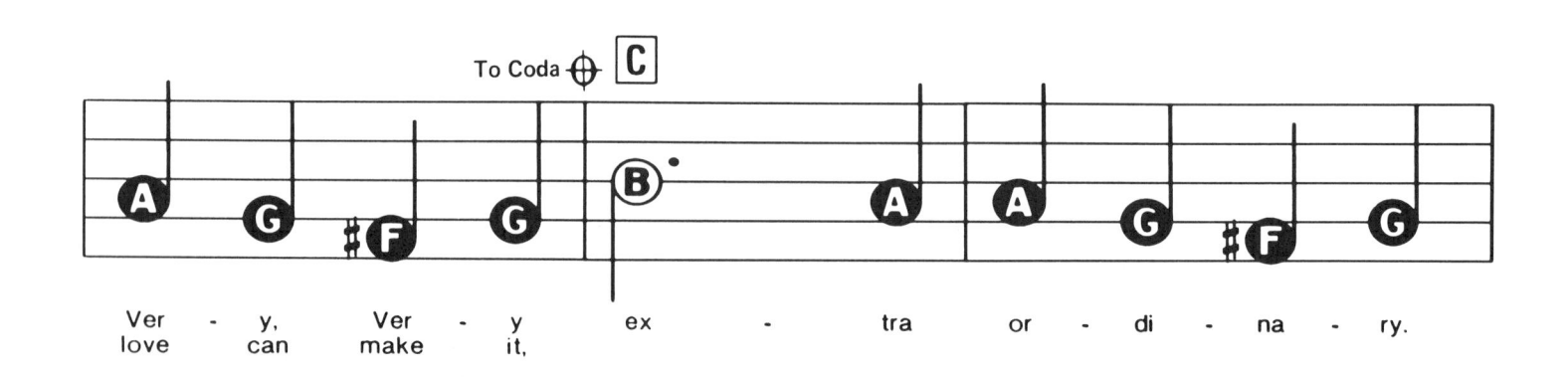

G — G· ♯F ♯F E ♯D E | D7 D — G· ♯F
Love L is for the way you Look at
you, is all that I can give to

♯F ♯F· E E D ♯C D
me, O is for more the On - ly
you, Love is than just a

G — ♯F· E E | G7 — B· A
one I see. V is
game for two, Two in

To Coda ⊕ C
A G ♯F G B· A A G ♯F G
Ver - y, Ver - y ex - tra - or - di - na - ry.
love can make it,

© 1964 (Renewed 1992) EDITION DOMA BERT KAEMPFERT
All Rights for the world excluding Germany, Austria and Switzerland Controlled and Administered by SCREEN GEMS-EMI MUSIC INC.
All Rights Reserved International Copyright Secured Used by Permission

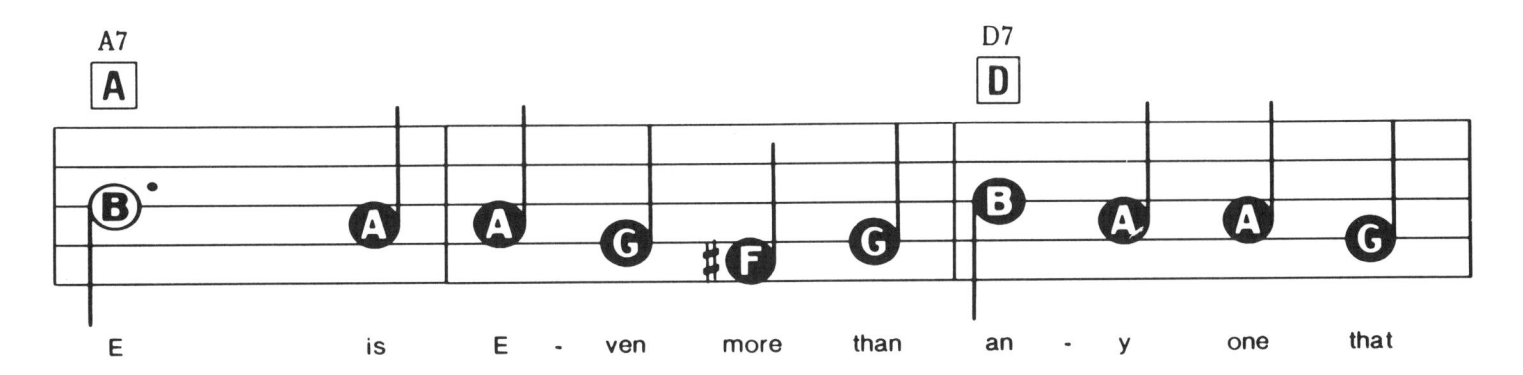

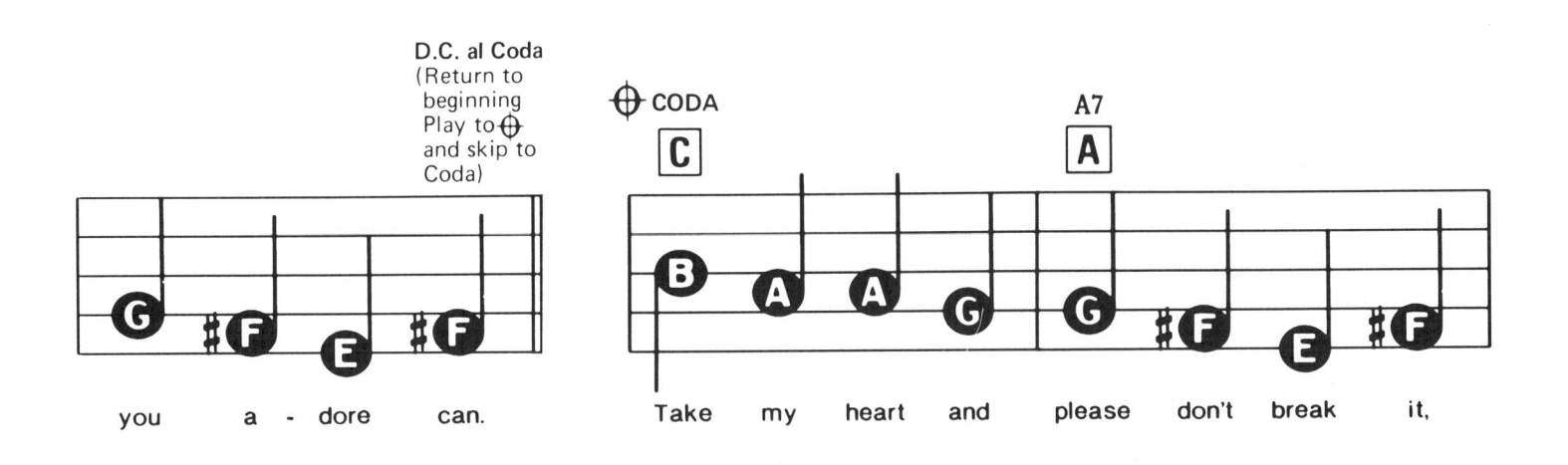

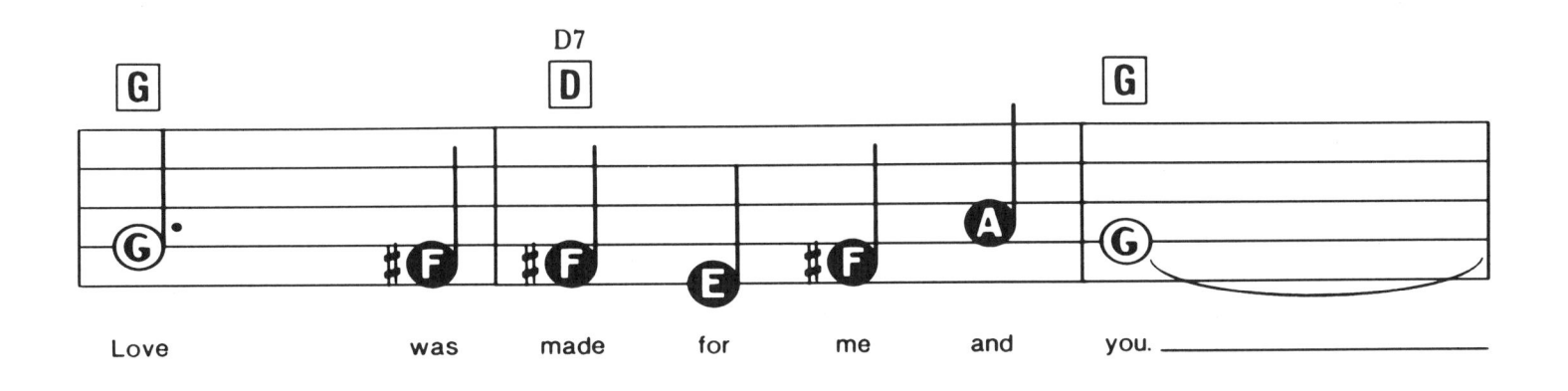

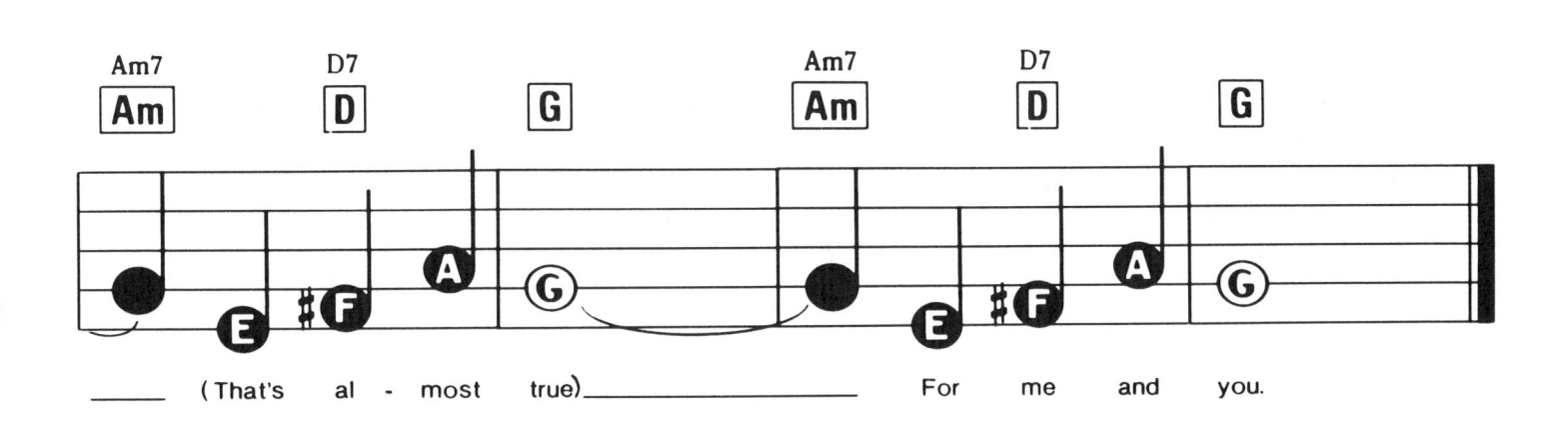

A7		D7	
A		**D**	

E is E- ven more than an-y one that

D.C. al Coda
(Return to beginning Play to ⊕ and skip to Coda)

you a- dore can.

⊕ CODA

	A7
C	**A**

Take my heart and please don't break it,

G	D7		G
G	**D**		**G**

Love was made for me and you. _____

Am7	D7	G	Am7	D7	G
Am	**D**	**G**	**Am**	**D**	**G**

_____ (That's al- most true) _____ For me and you.

Mambo #5

Registration 1
Rhythm: Mambo or Latin

Words and Music by
Damaso Perez Prado

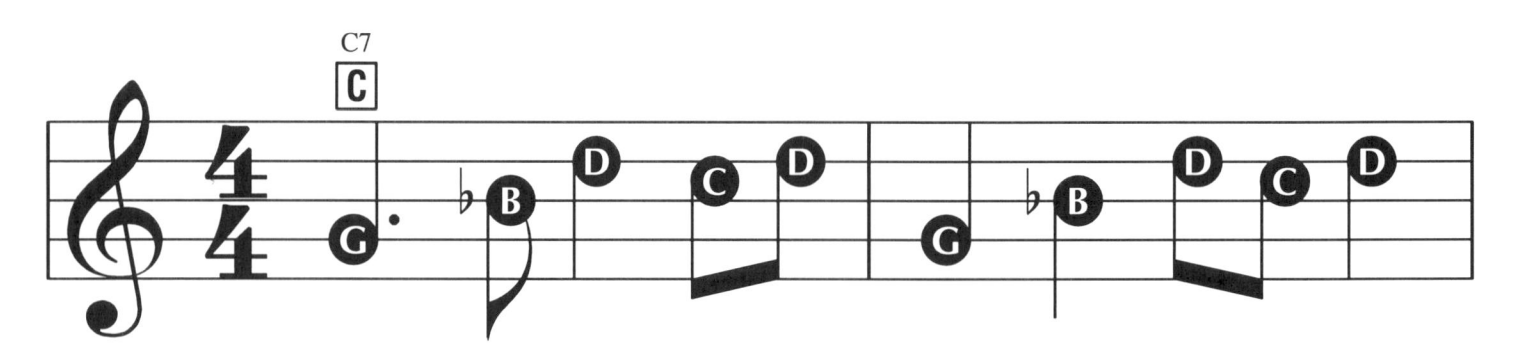

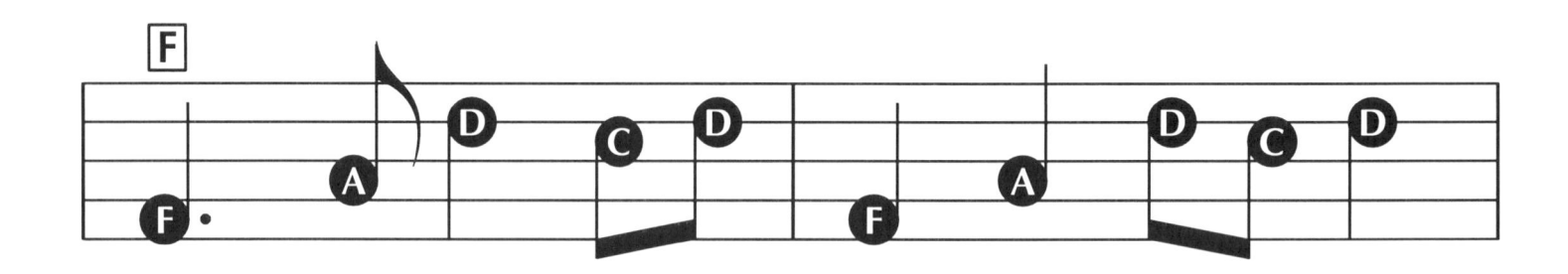

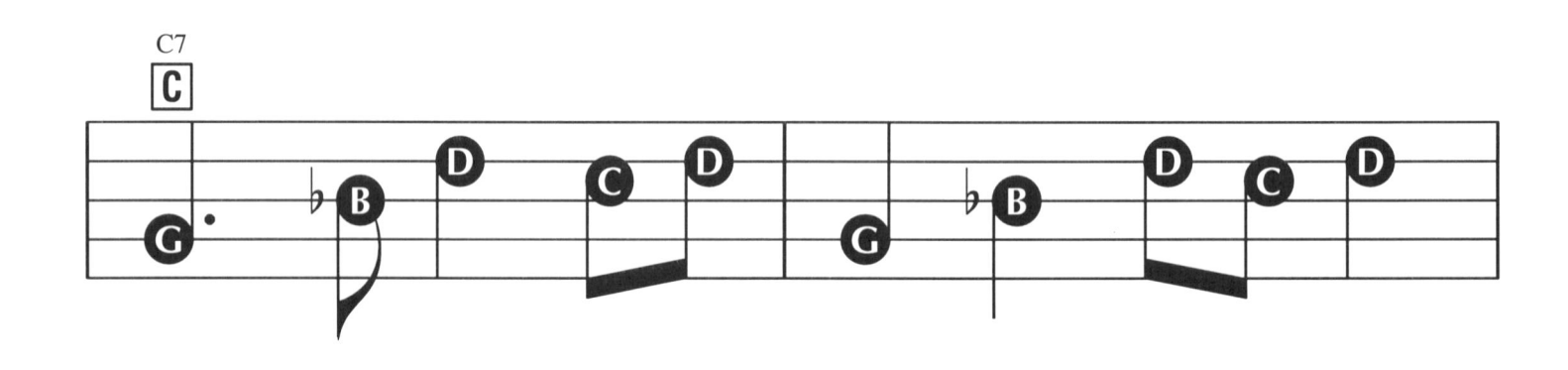

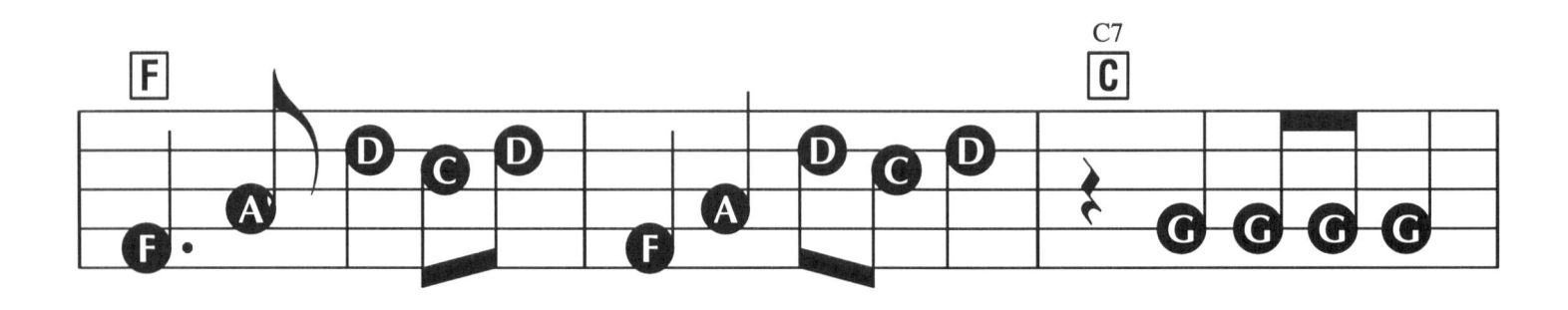

Copyright © 1948 by Editorial Mexicana de Musica Internacional, S.A.
Copyright Renewed
All Rights Administered by Peer International Corporation
International Copyright Secured   All Rights Reserved

45

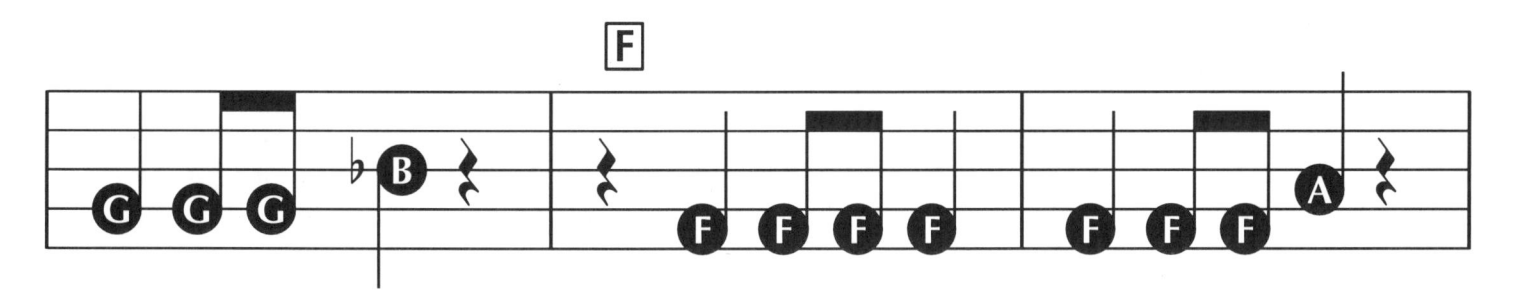

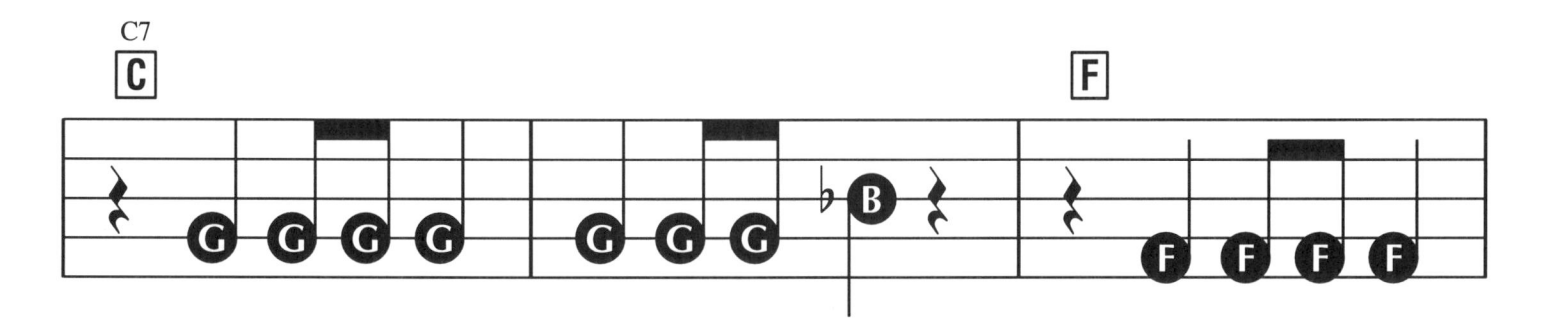

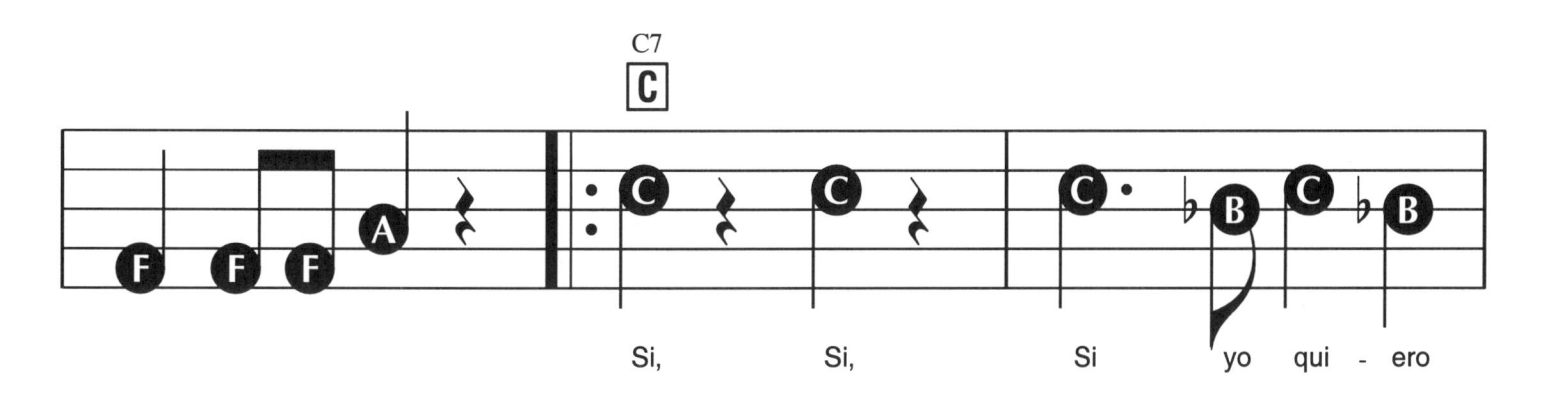

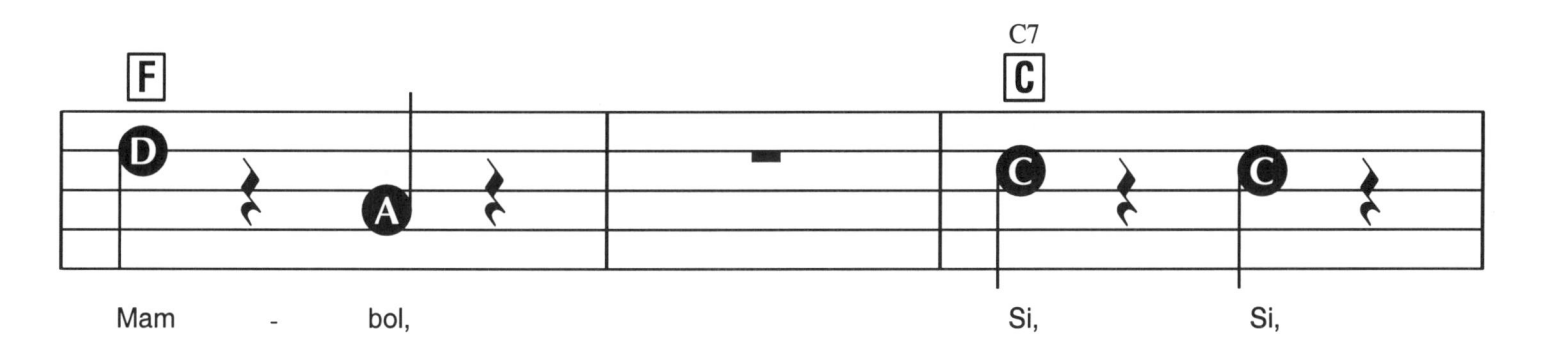

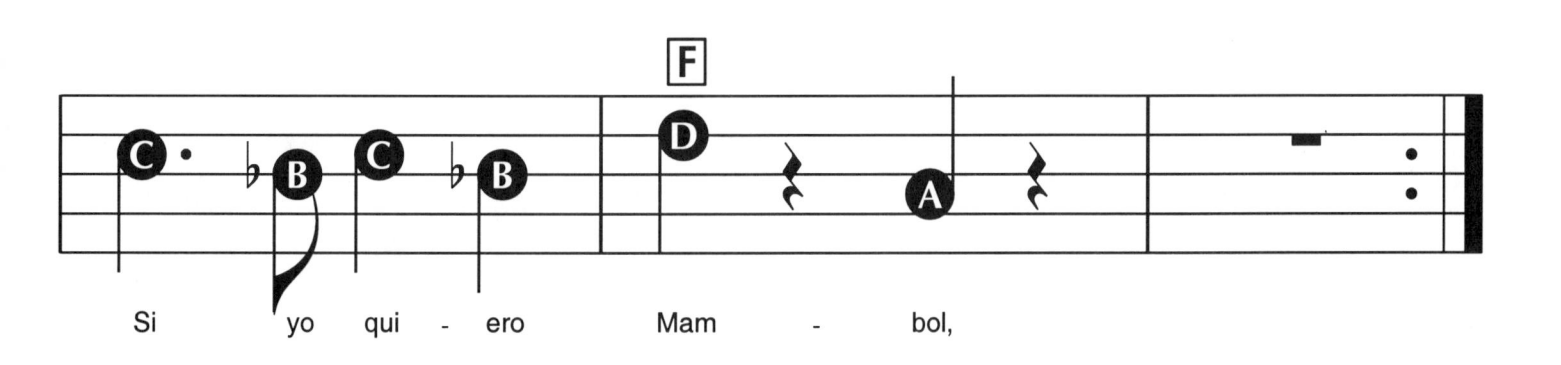

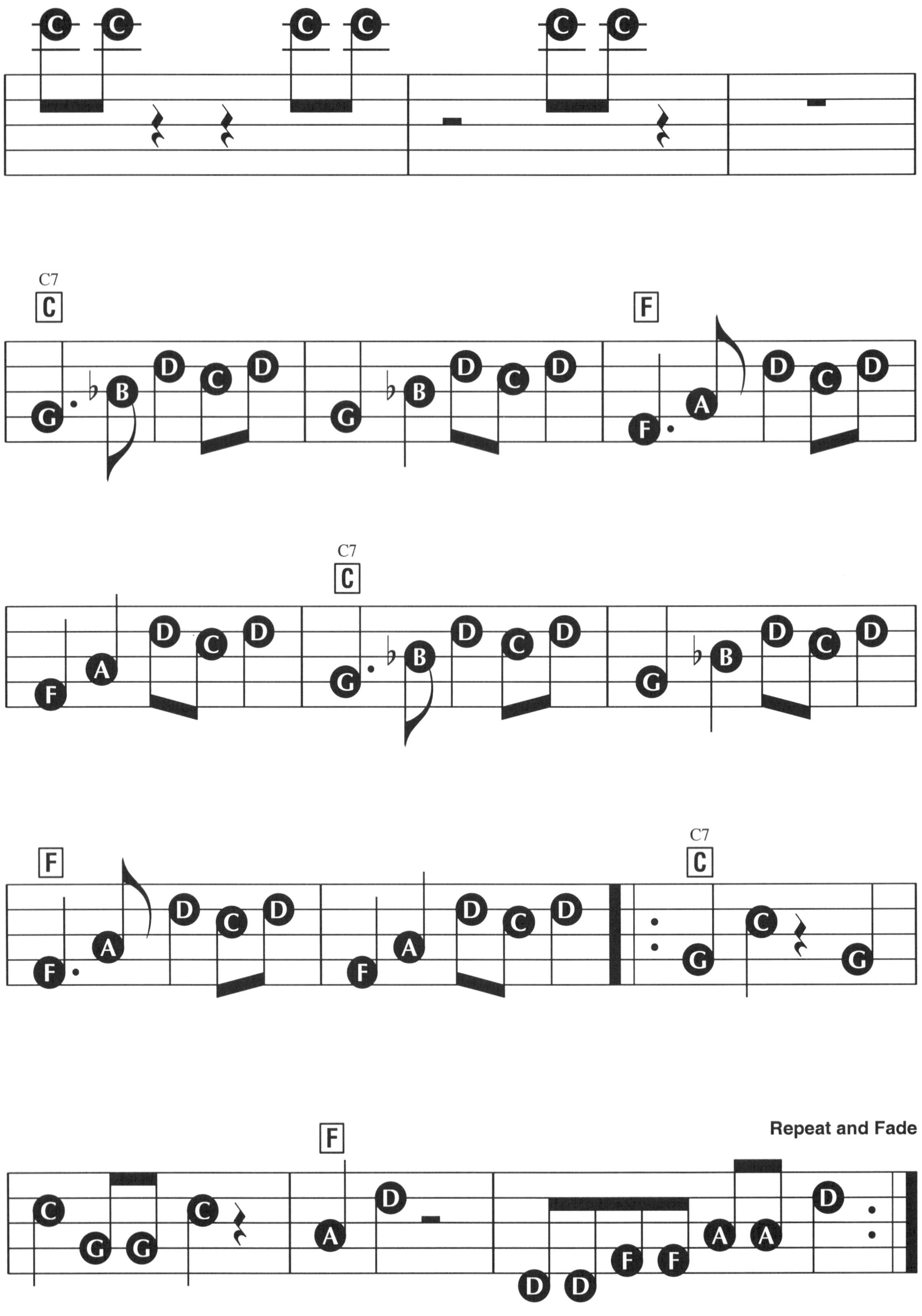
C7
C
F
C7
C
F
C7
C
Repeat and Fade
F

Spanish Eyes

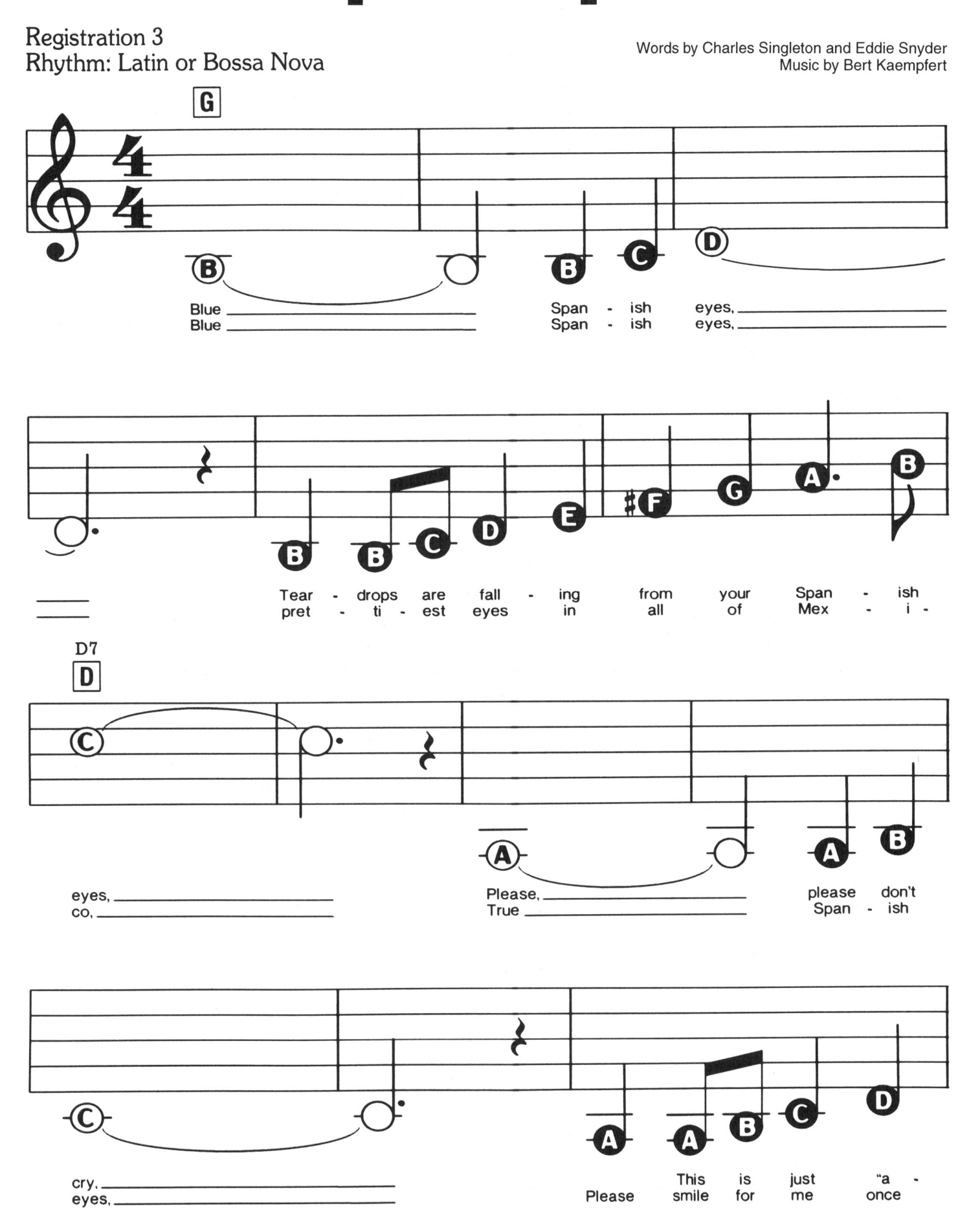

Registration 3
Rhythm: Latin or Bossa Nova

Words by Charles Singleton and Eddie Snyder
Music by Bert Kaempfert

Blue _____ Span-ish eyes, _____
Blue _____ Span-ish eyes, _____

_____ Tear-drops are fall-ing from your Span-ish
_____ pret-ti-est eyes in all of Mex-i-

eyes, _____ Please, _____ please don't
co, _____ True _____ Span-ish

cry, _____ Please This smile is just for me "a
eyes, _____ once

© 1965, 1966 (Renewed 1993, 1994) EDITION DOMA BERT KAEMPFERT
All Rights for the world, excluding Germany, Austria and Switzerland, Controlled and Administered by SCREEN GEMS-EMI MUSIC INC.
All Rights Reserved International Copyright Secured Used by Permission

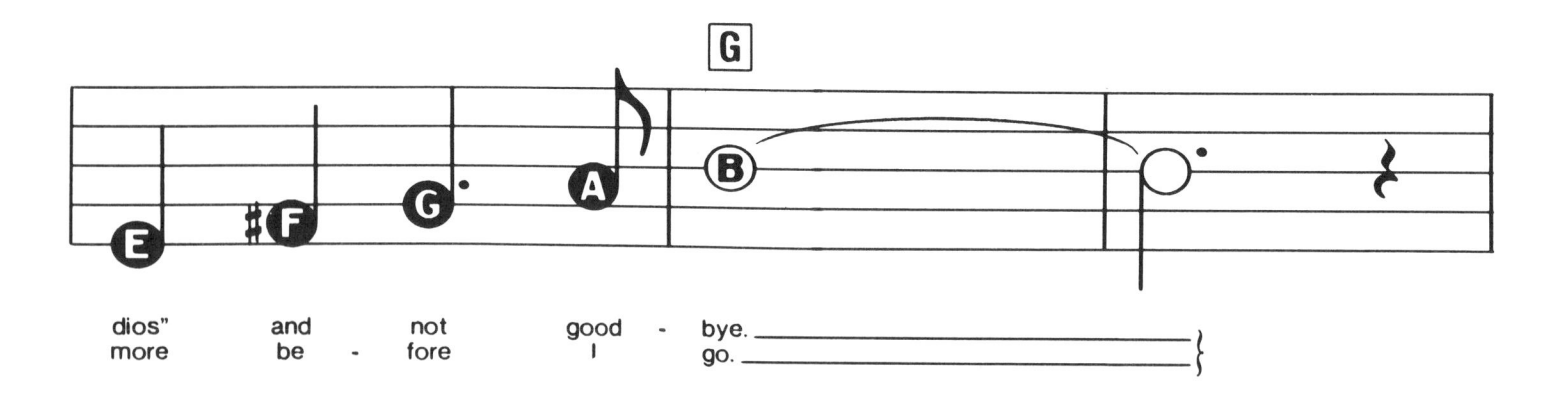

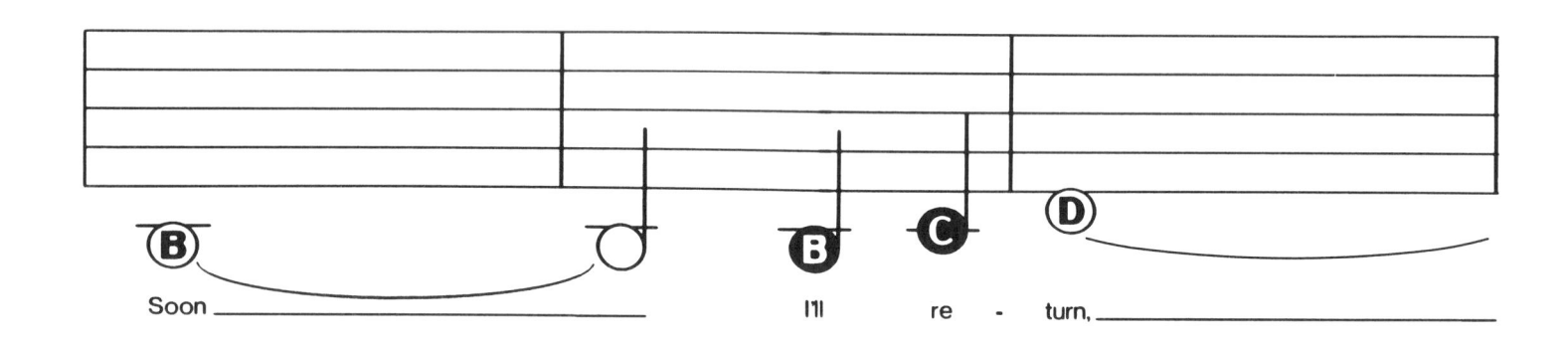

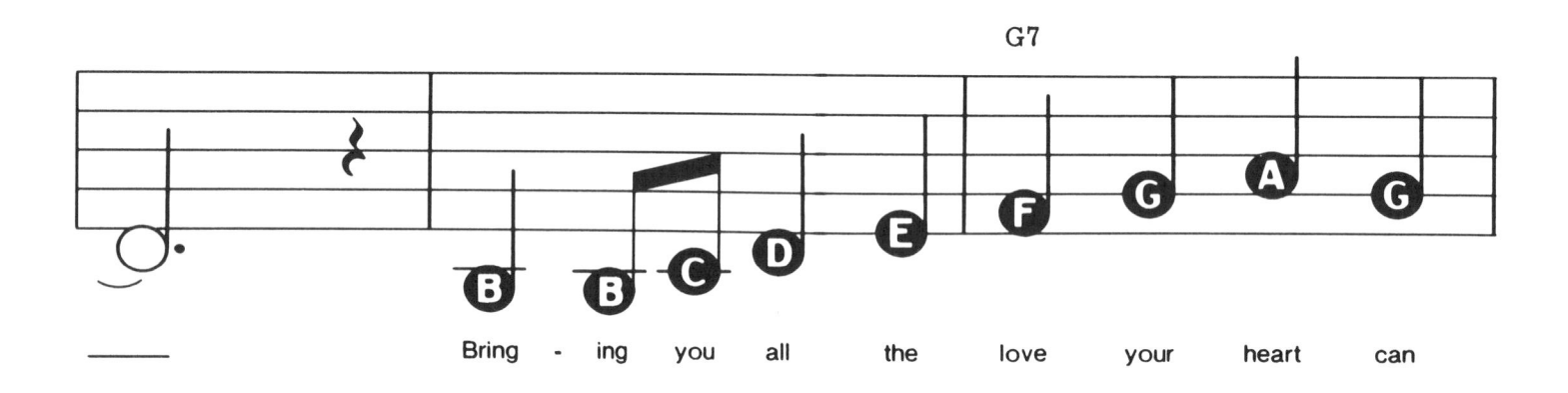

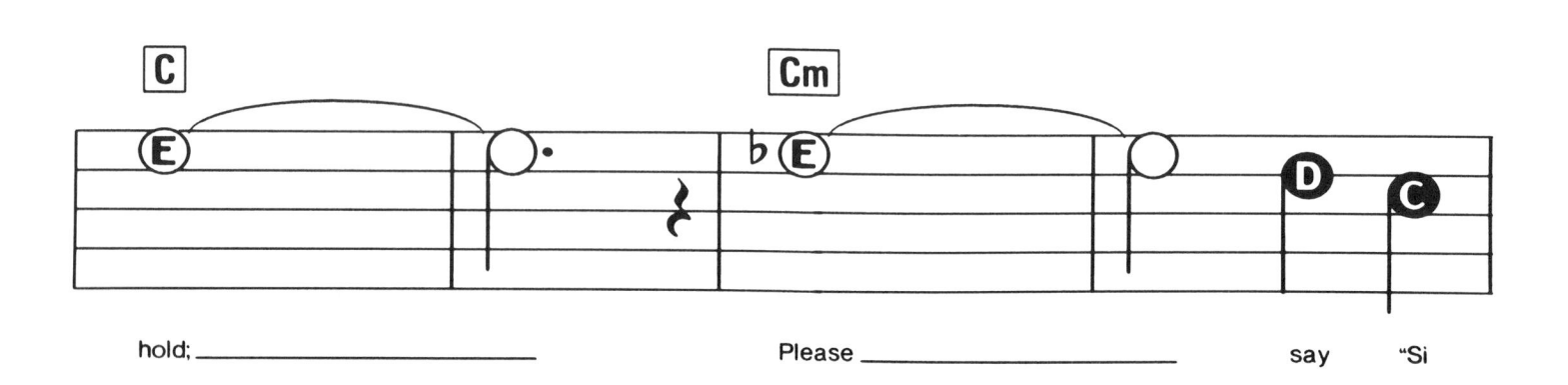

dios" and not good - bye.
more be - fore I go.

Soon _____ I'll re - turn,

Bring - ing you all the love your heart can

hold; Please say "Si

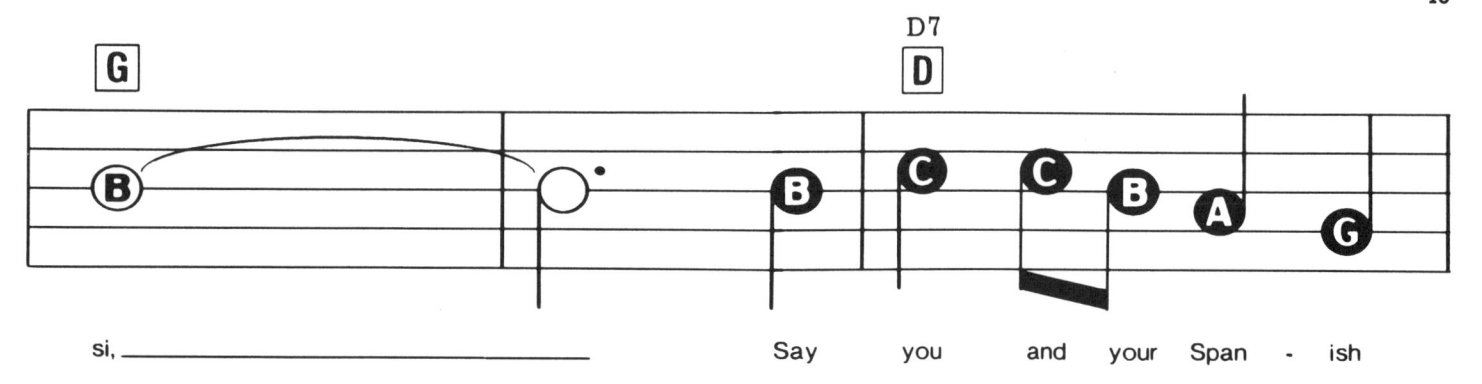

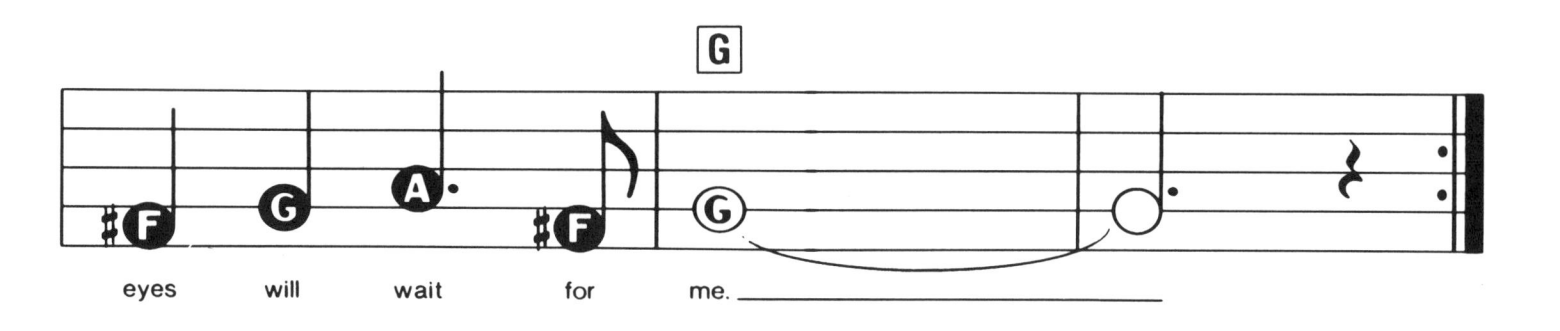

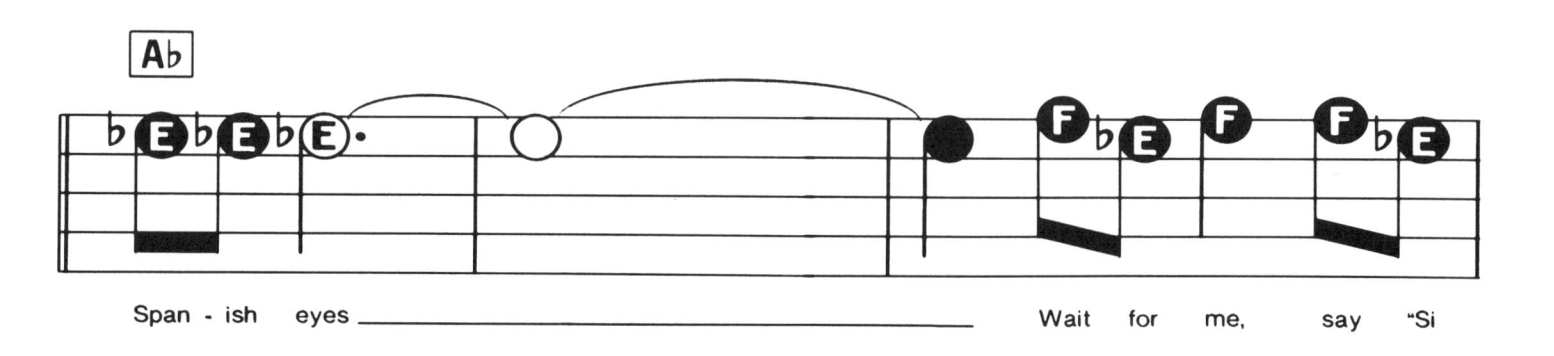

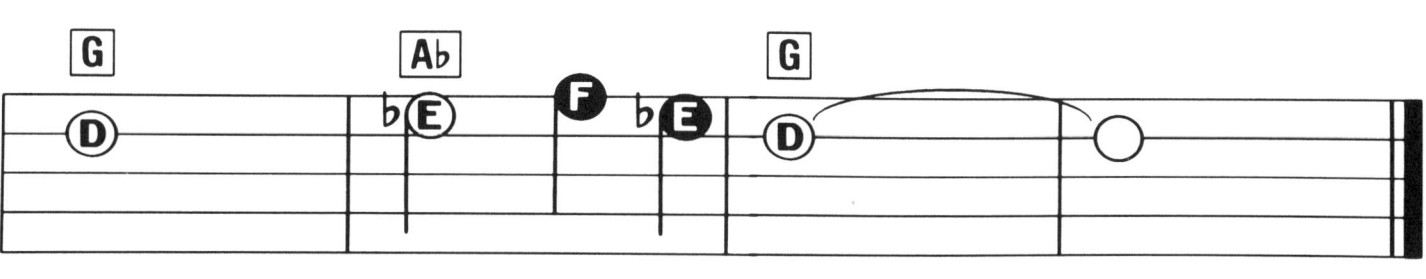

si, _____ Say you and your Span - ish eyes will wait for me. _____ Span - ish eyes _____ Wait for me, say "Si Si!" _____

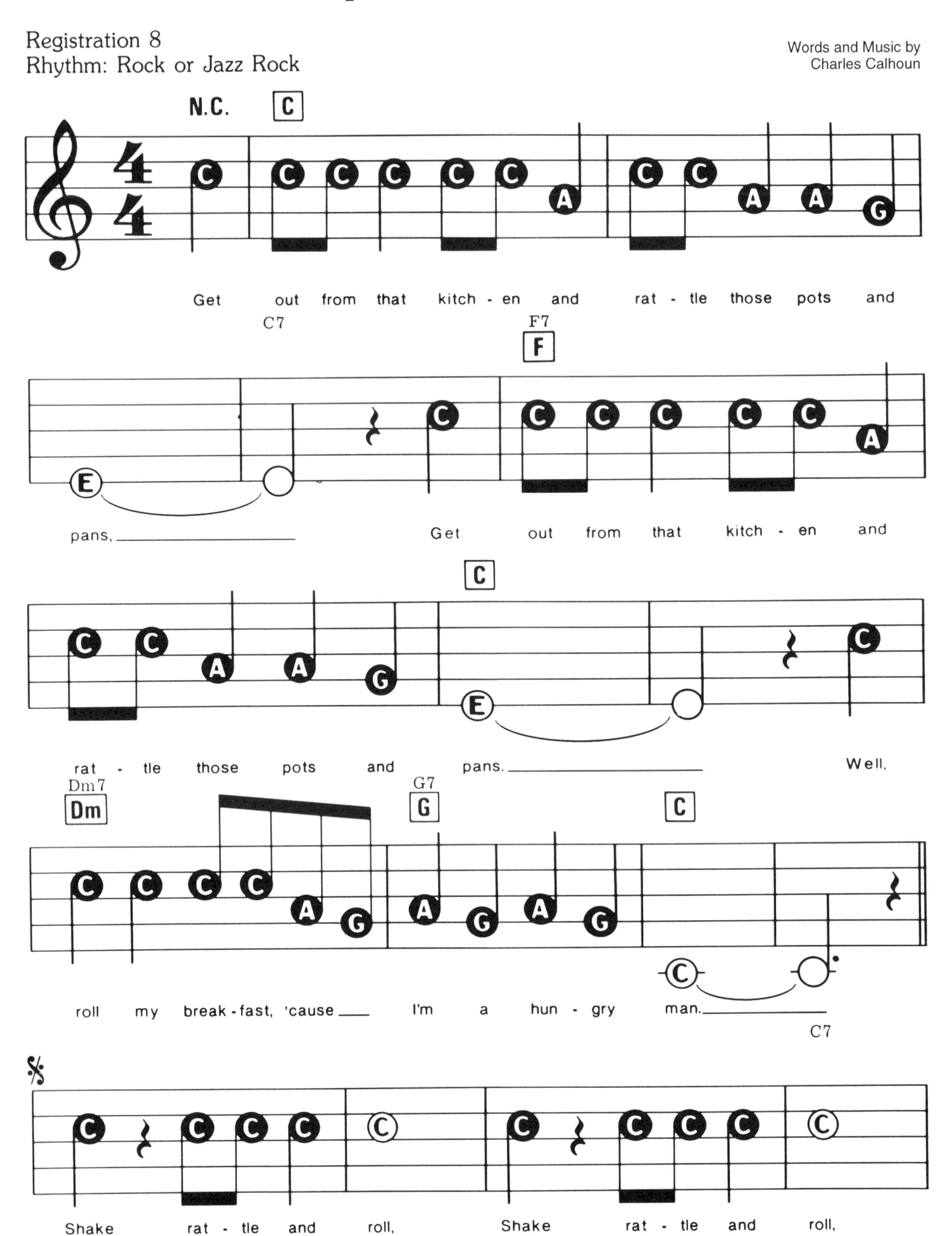

Shake, Rattle and Roll

Registration 8
Rhythm: Rock or Jazz Rock

Words and Music by
Charles Calhoun

Get out from that kitch-en and rat-tle those pots and pans,_____ Get out from that kitch-en and rat-tle those pots and pans._____ Well, roll my break-fast, 'cause____ I'm a hun-gry man._____

Shake rat-tle and roll, Shake rat-tle and roll,

Copyright © 1954 by Unichappell Music Inc.
Copyright Renewed
International Copyright Secured   All Rights Reserved

Shake rat-tle and roll, Shake rat-tle and roll; You nev-er do noth-in to save your dog-gone soul.

Wear-in' those dress-es, your hair done up so right,

Wear-in' those dress-es, your hair done up so right; You look so warm, but your heart is cold as ice.

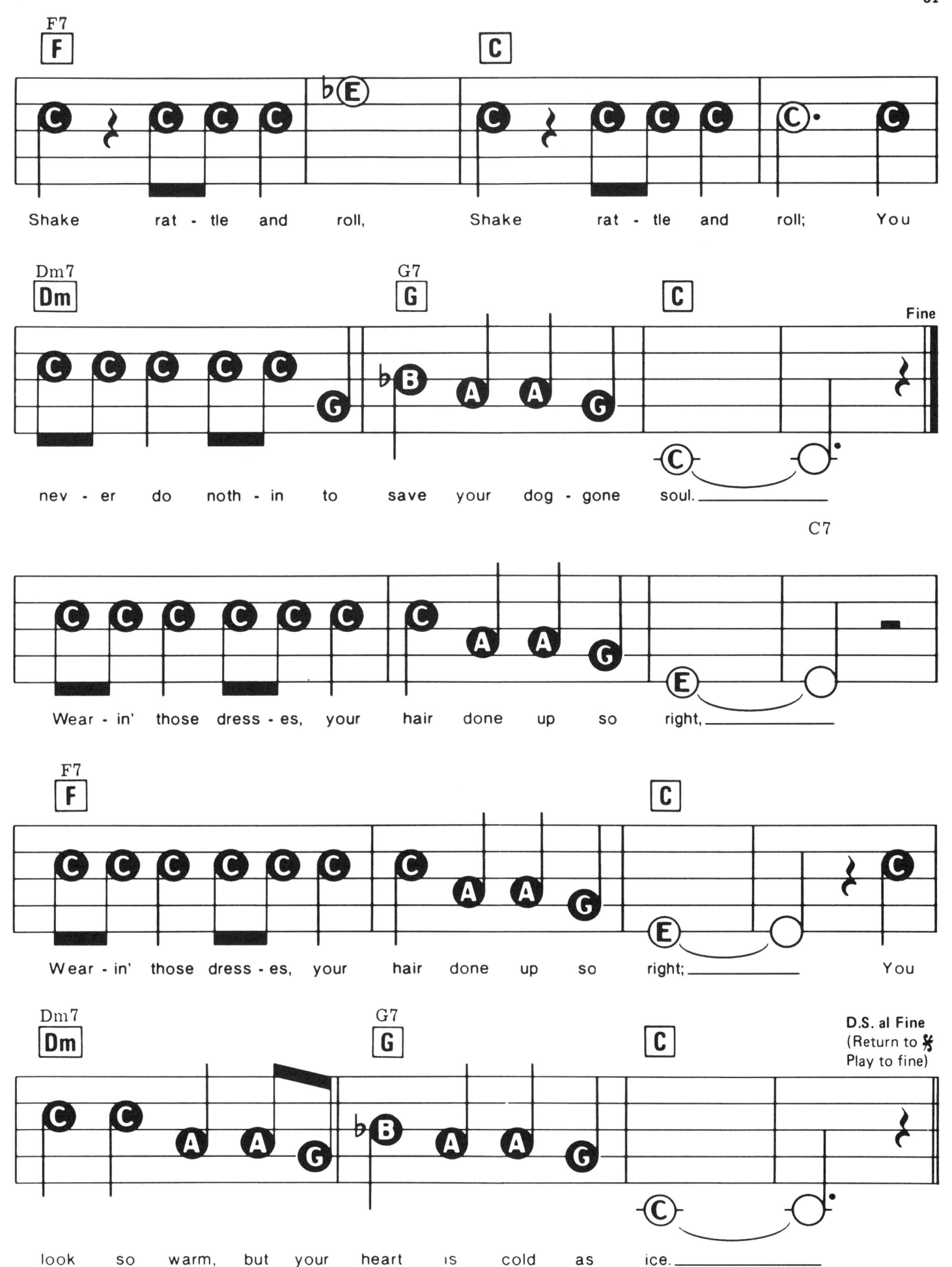

D.S. al Fine (Return to 𝄋 Play to fine)

A String of Pearls
from THE GLENN MILLER STORY

Registration 4
Rhythm: Swing

Words by Eddie De Lange
Music by Jerry Gray

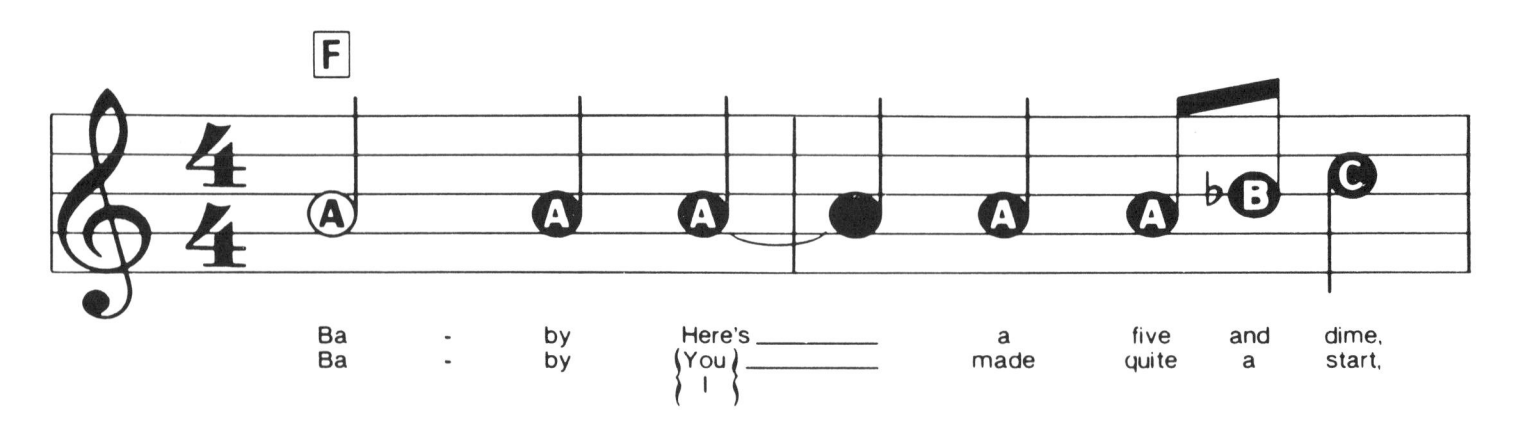

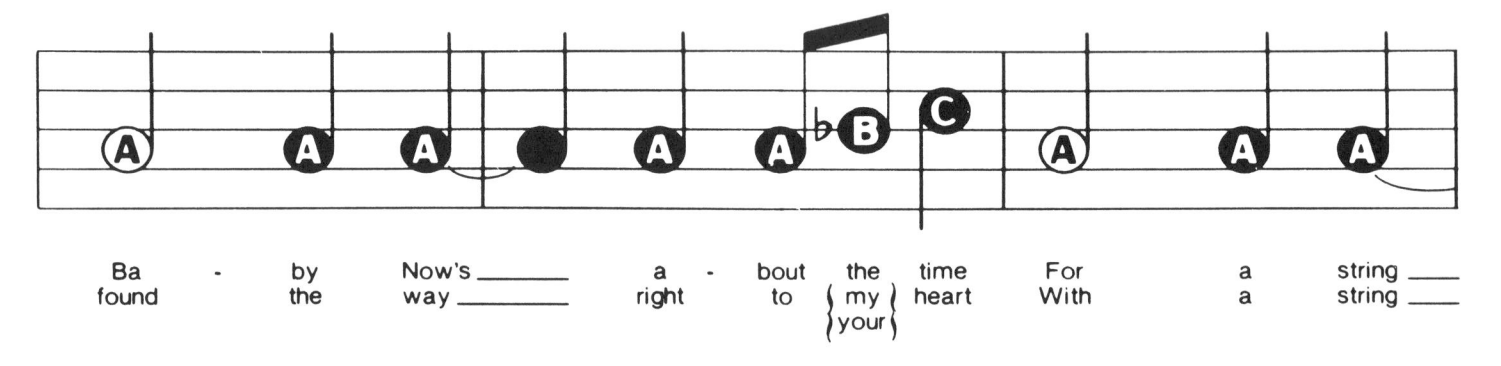

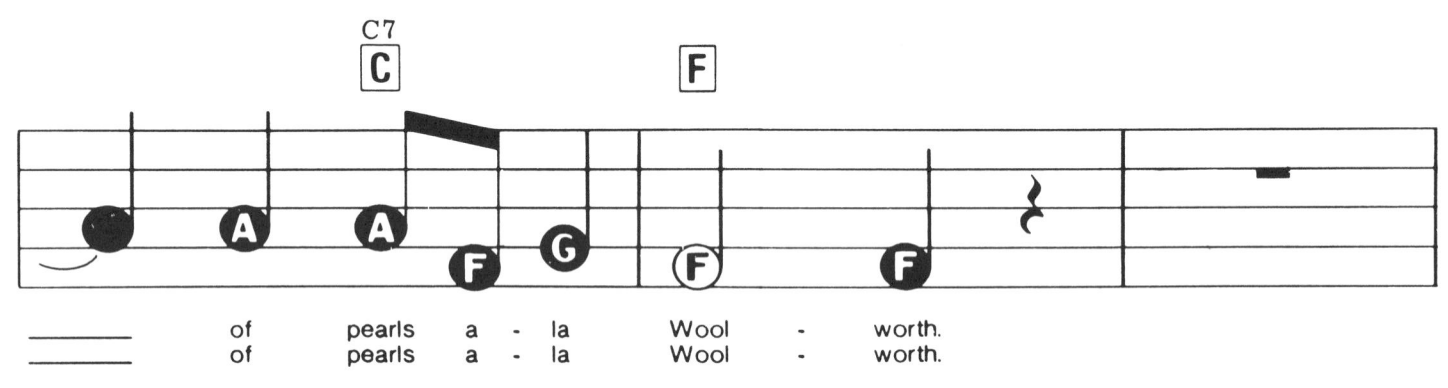

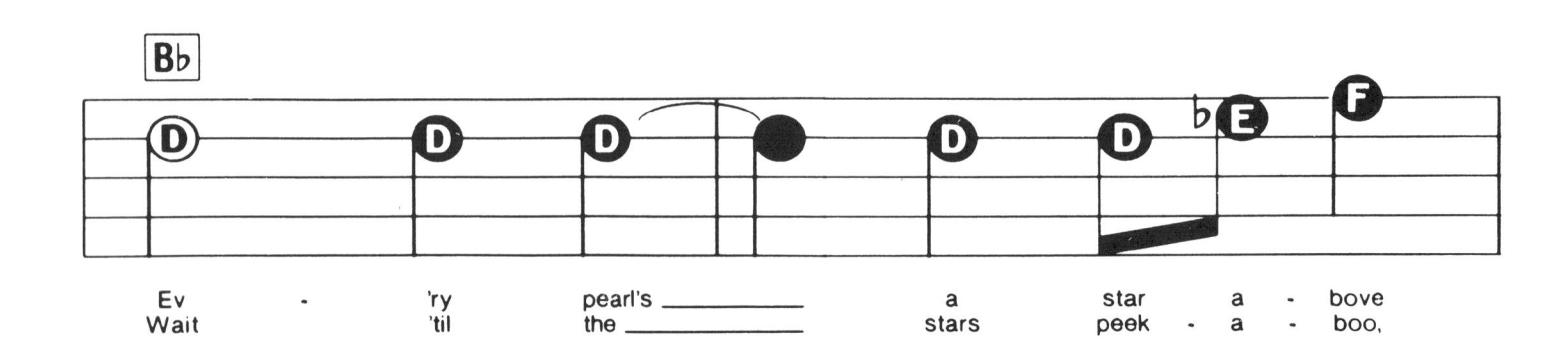

Ba - by Here's _____ a five and dime,
Ba - by (You) _____ made quite a start,
     (I)

Ba - by Now's _____ a - bout the time For a string _____
found the way _____ right to (my) heart With a string _____
                              (your)

_____ of pearls a - la Wool - worth.
_____ of pearls a - la Wool - worth.

Ev - 'ry pearl's _____ a star a - bove
Wait 'til the _____ stars peek - a - boo,

Copyright © 1941, 1942 by Mutual Music Society, Inc.
Copyright Renewed, Assigned to Chappell & Co. and Scarsdale Music Corp.
International Copyright Secured   All Rights Reserved

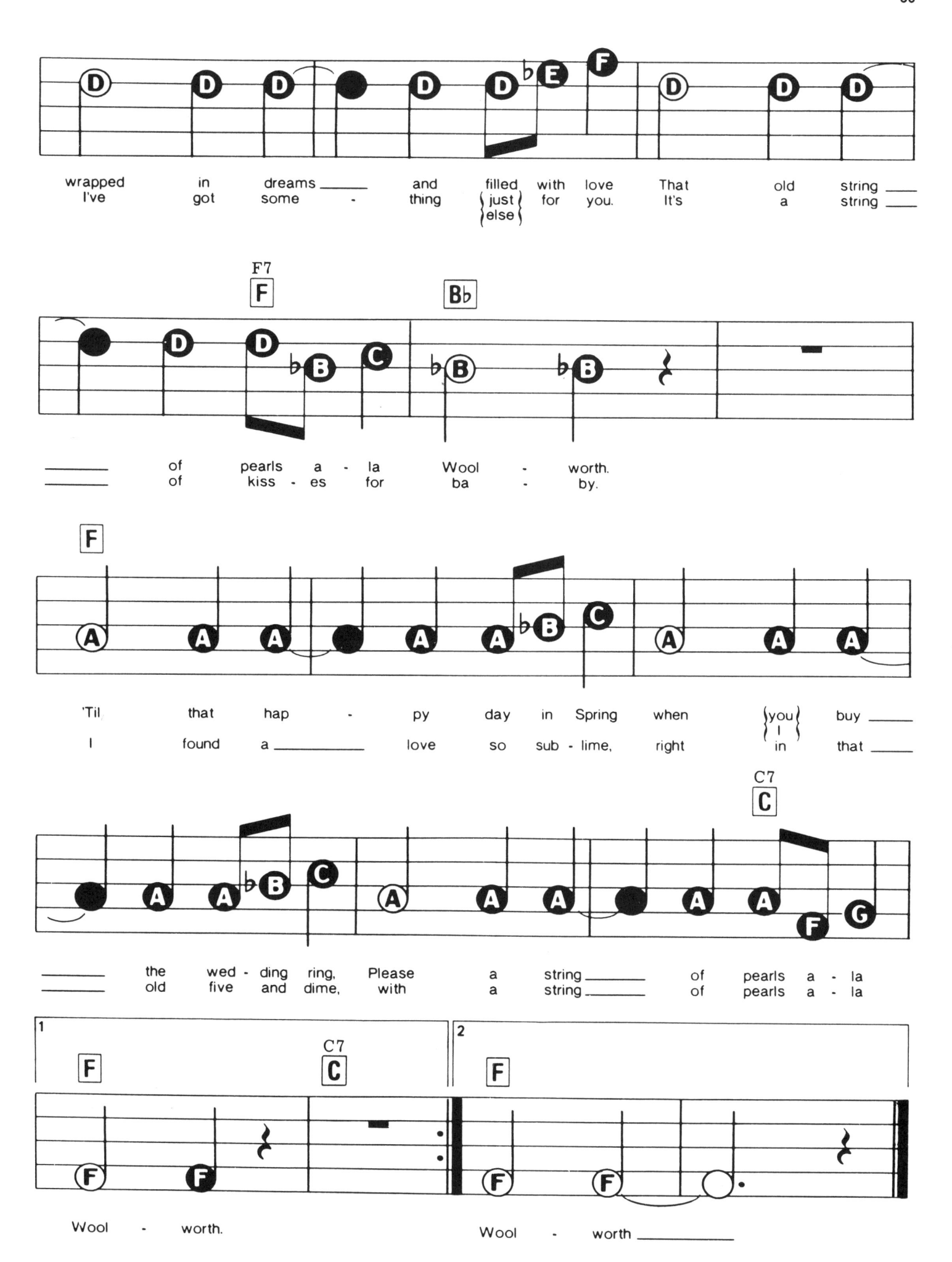

wrapped in dreams ___ and filled with love. That old string ___
I've got some-thing {just/else} for you. It's a string ___

___ of pearls a-la Wool-worth.
___ of kiss-es for ba-by.

'Til that hap-py day in Spring when {you/I} buy ___
I found a ___ love so sub-lime, right in that ___

___ the wed-ding ring, Please a string ___ of pearls a-la
___ old five and dime, with a string ___ of pearls a-la

Wool-worth. Wool-worth ___

Tennessee Waltz

Registration 4
Rhythm: Waltz

Words and Music by Redd Stewart
and Pee Wee King

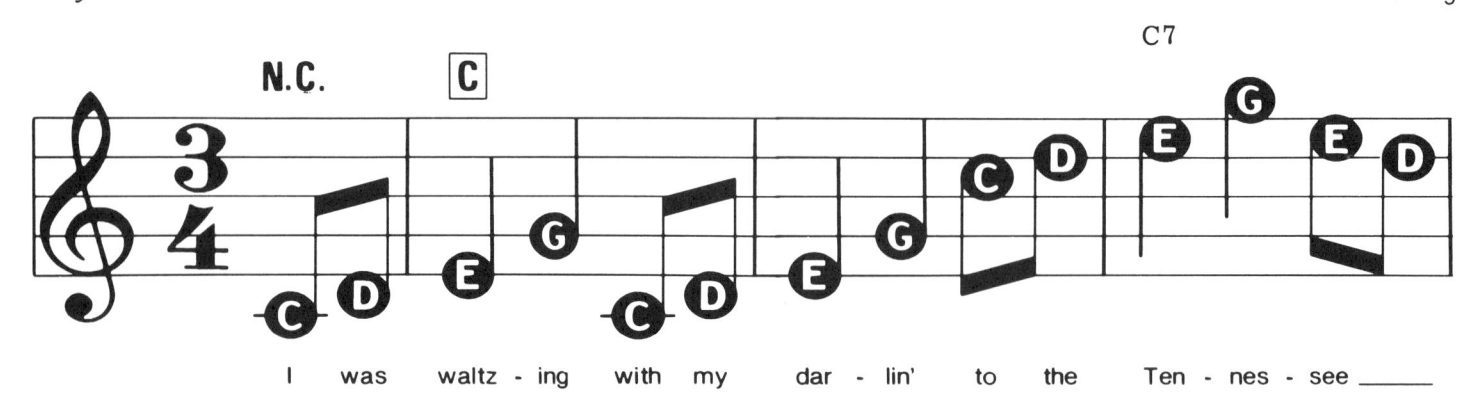

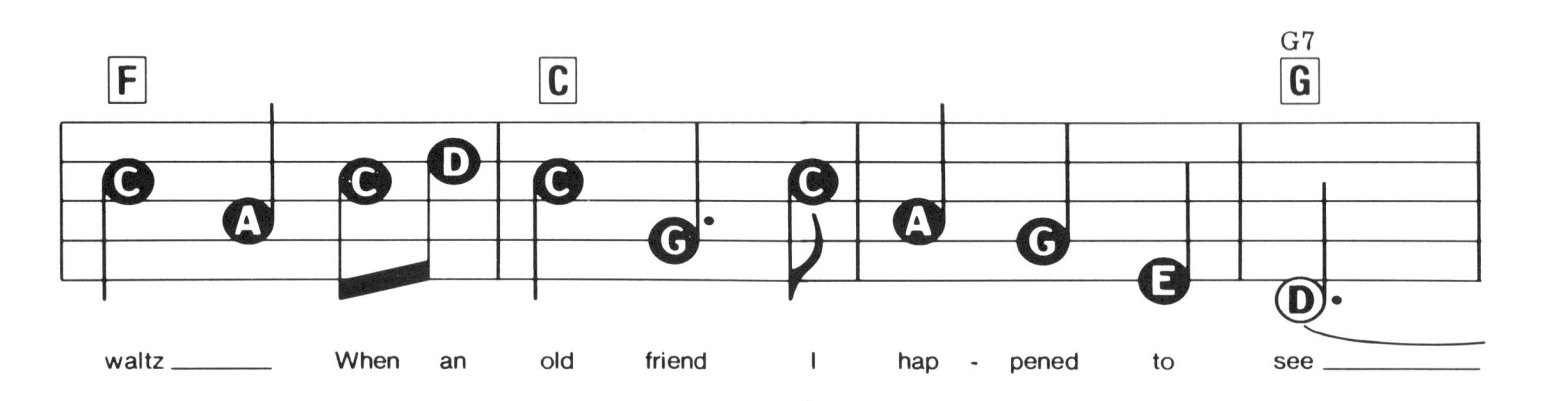

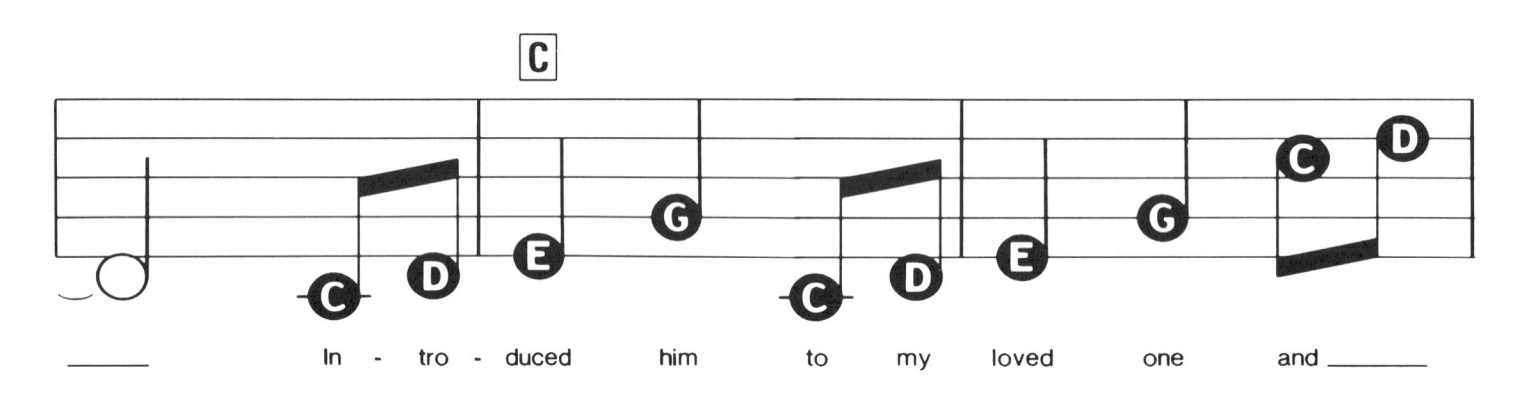

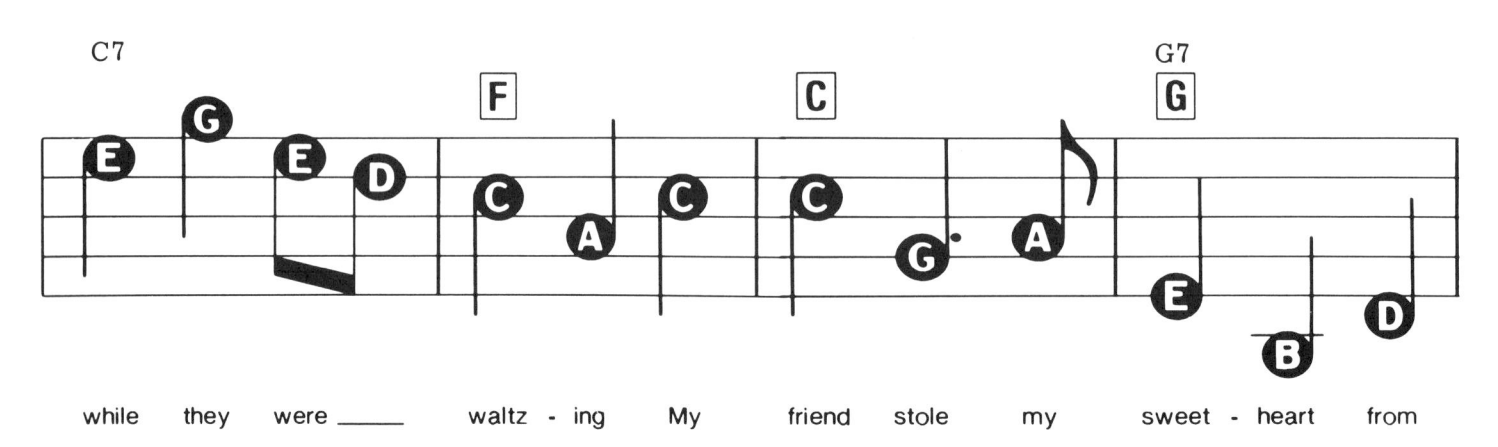

I was waltz - ing with my dar - lin' to the Ten - nes - see waltz When an old friend I hap - pened to see In - tro - duced him to my loved one and while they were waltz - ing My friend stole my sweet - heart from

Copyright © 1948 (Renewed 1975) by Acuff-Rose Music, Inc.
All Rights Reserved   Used by Permission

55

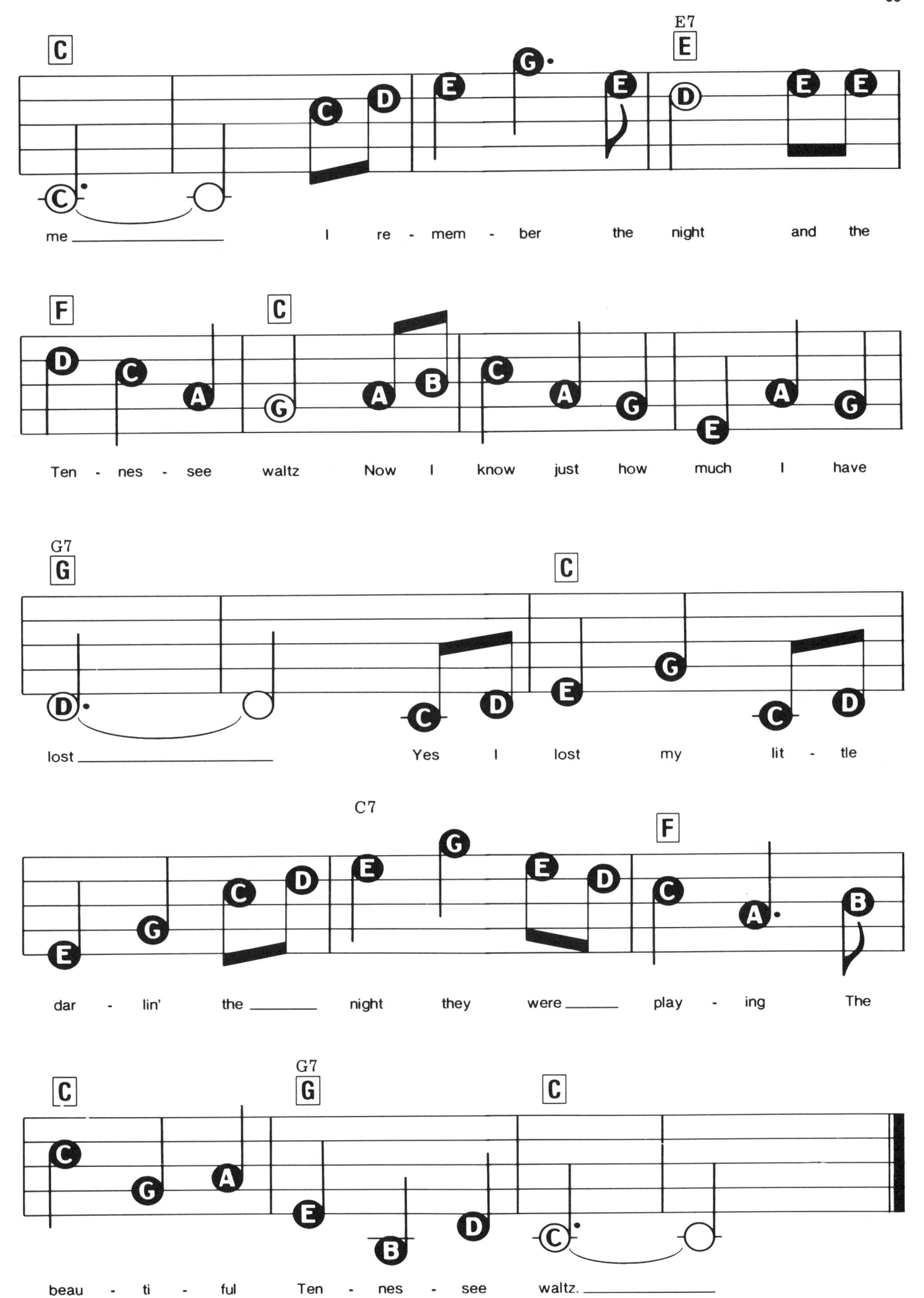

me _____ I re - mem - ber the night and the Ten - nes - see waltz Now I know just how much I have lost _____ Yes I lost my lit - tle dar - lin' the _____ night they were _____ play - ing The beau - ti - ful Ten - nes - see waltz. _____

Twilight Time

Registration 9
Rhythm: Ballad or Fox Trot

Lyric by Buck Ram
Music by Morty Nevins and Al Nevins

Heav - en - ly shades of night are fall - ing, It's twi - light time.
Deep - en - ing shad - ows gath - er splen - dor as day is done.
Deep in the dark your kiss will thrill me like days of old,

Out of the mist your voice is call - ing, It's twi - light time.
Fin - gers of night will soon sur - ren - der the set - ting sun.
Light - ing the spark of love that fills me with dreams un - told.

When pur - ple col - ored cur - tains mark the end of day. I
I count the mo - ments, dar - ling till you're here with me, To -
Each day I pray for eve - ning just to be with you, To -

hear you, my dear, at twi - light time.

TRO - © Copyright 1944 (Renewed) Devon Music, Inc., New York, NY
International Copyright Secured
All Rights Reserved Including Public Performance For Profit
Used by Permission

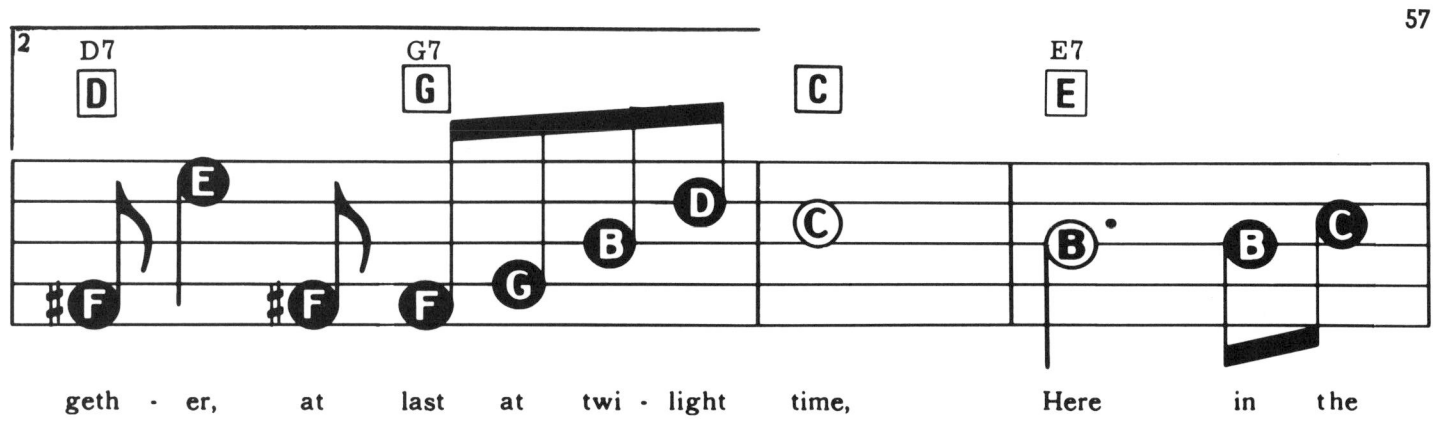

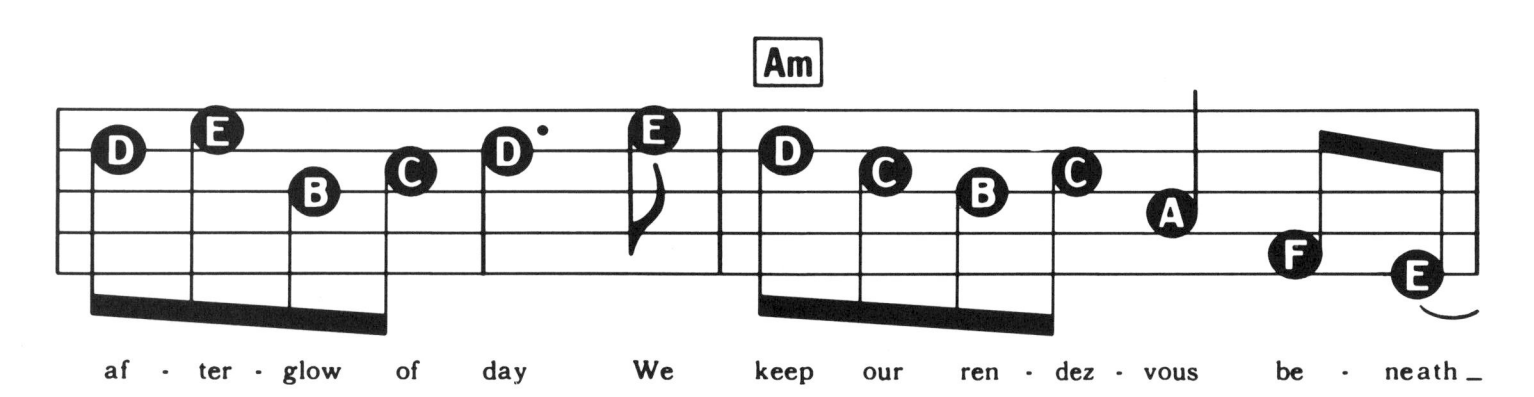

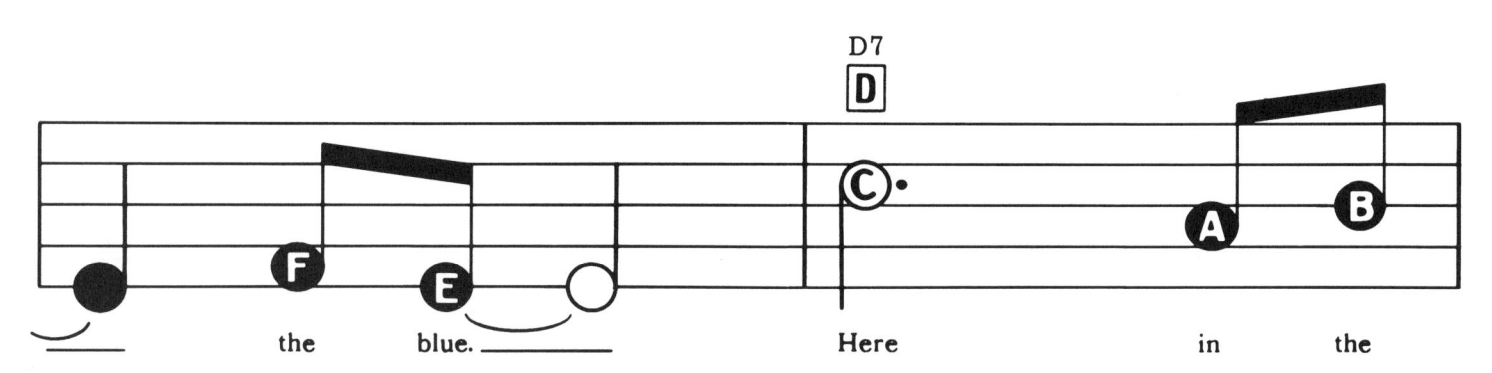

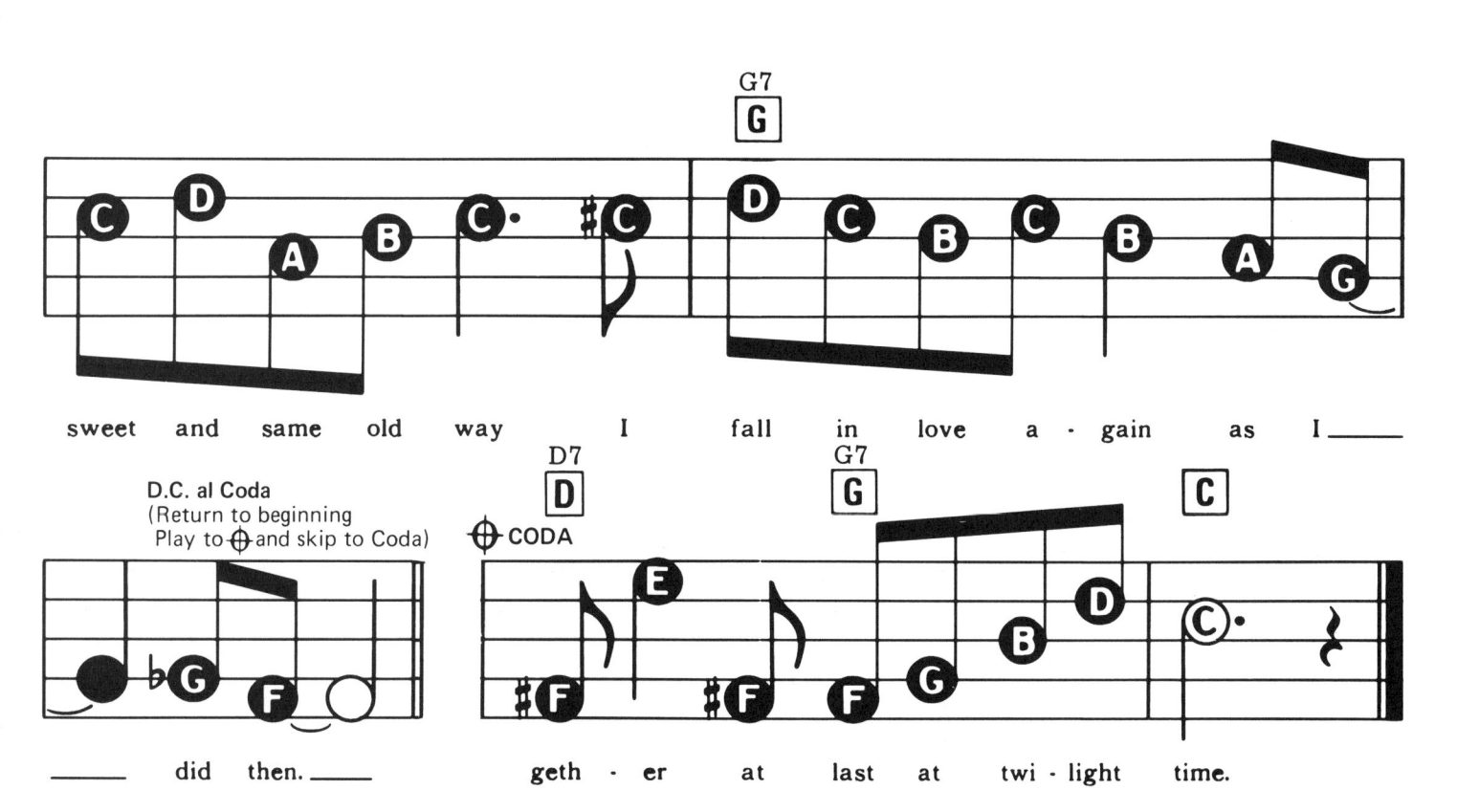

geth - er, at last at twi - light time, Here in the af - ter - glow of day We keep our ren - dez - vous be - neath the blue. Here in the sweet and same old way I fall in love a - gain as I did then. geth - er at last at twi - light time.

D.C. al Coda
(Return to beginning
Play to ⊕ and skip to Coda)

⊕ CODA

The Twist

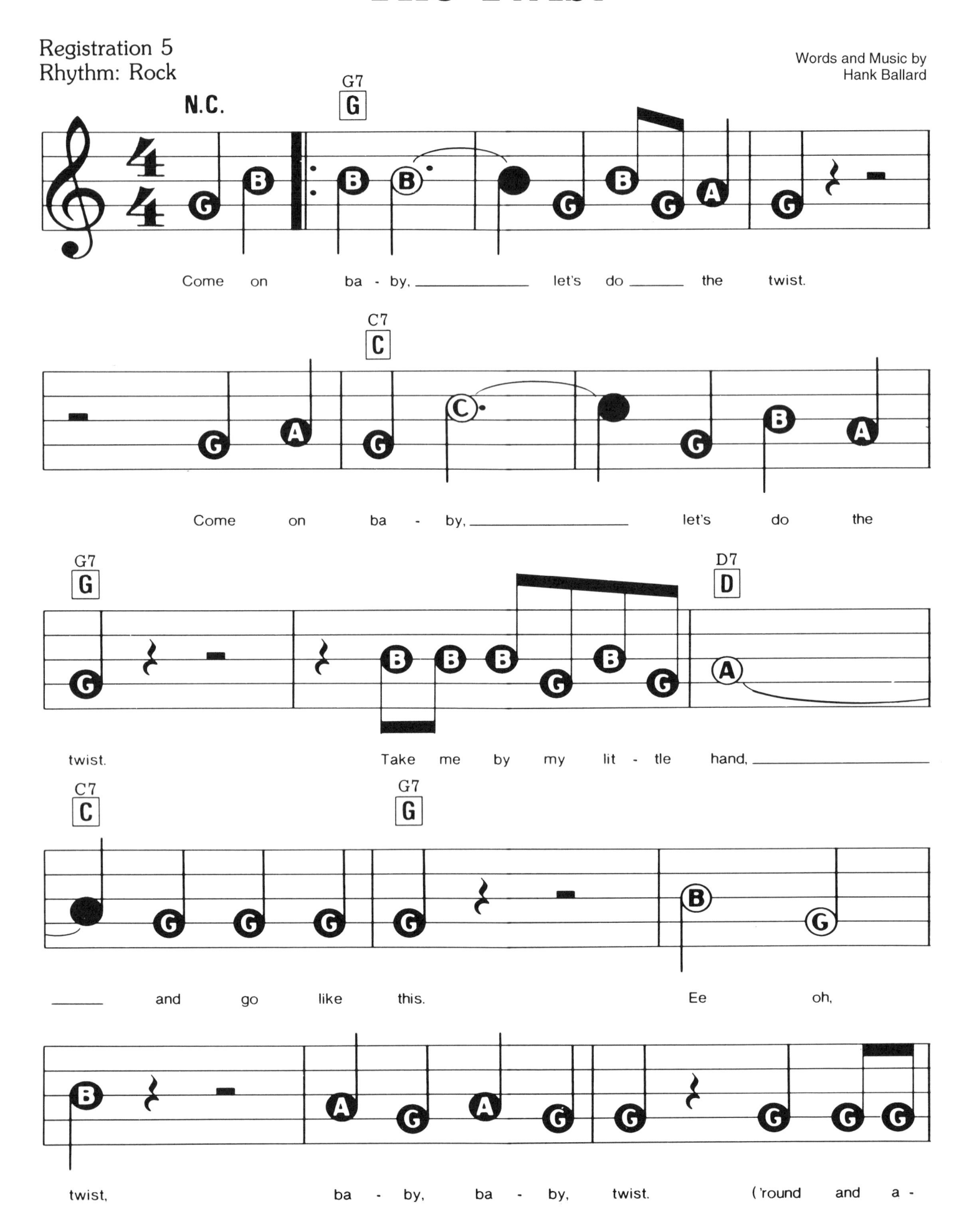

Registration 5
Rhythm: Rock

Words and Music by
Hank Ballard

Come on ba - by, let's do the twist.

Come on ba - by, let's do the twist. Take me by my lit - tle hand, and go like this. Ee oh, twist, ba - by, ba - by, twist. ('round and a-

Copyright © 1958 by Fort Knox Music Inc. and Trio Music Company, Inc.
Copyright Renewed
International Copyright Secured   All Rights Reserved
Used by Permission

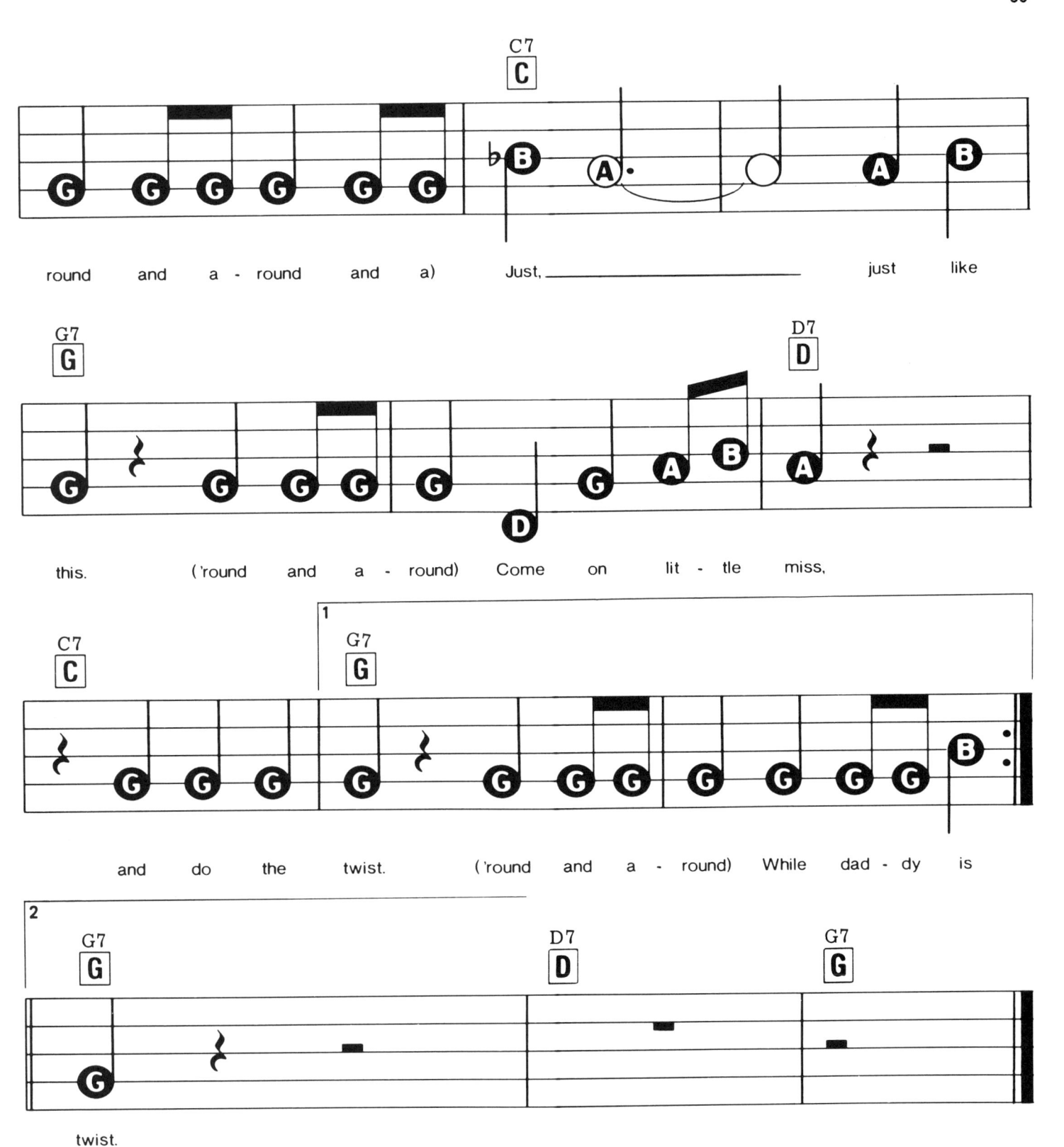

[C7] round and a-round and a) Just, _____ just like [G7] this. ('round and a-round) Come on lit-tle miss, [D7] [C7] and do the twist. ('round and a-round) While dad-dy is [G7] twist.

Verse 2
While daddy is sleeping and mama ain't around,
While daddy is sleeping and mama ain't around,
We're gonna twisty, twisty, twisty until we tear the house down.

You should see my little sis,
You should see my little sis,
She knows how to rock and she knows how to twist.

Where the Boys Are

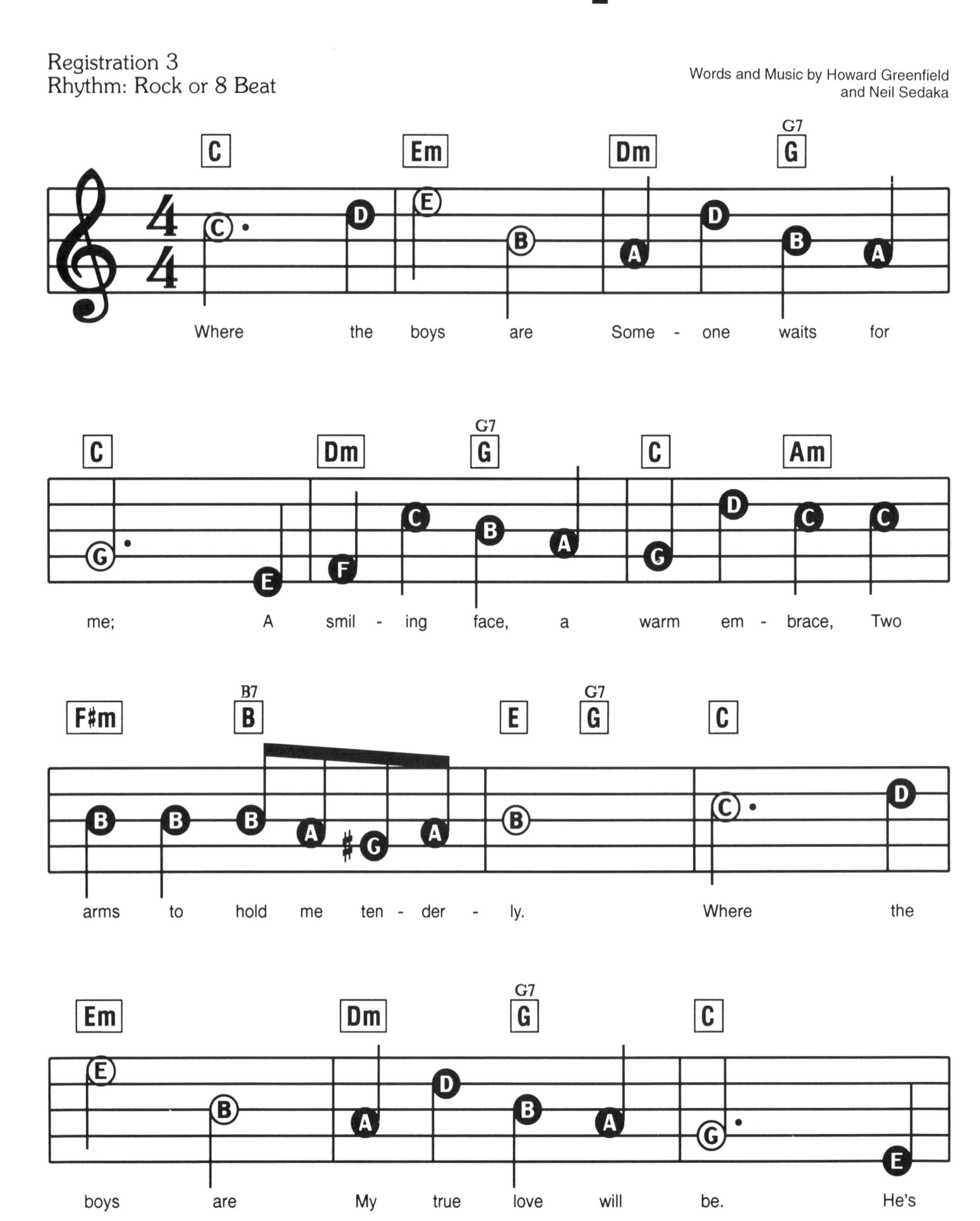

Registration 3
Rhythm: Rock or 8 Beat

Words and Music by Howard Greenfield
and Neil Sedaka

Where the boys are Some-one waits for me; A smil-ing face, a warm em-brace, Two arms to hold me ten-der-ly. Where the boys are My true love will be. He's

© 1960 (Renewed 1988) SCREEN GEMS-EMI MUSIC INC. and CAREERS-BMG MUSIC PUBLISHING, INC.
All Rights Reserved International Copyright Secured Used by Permission

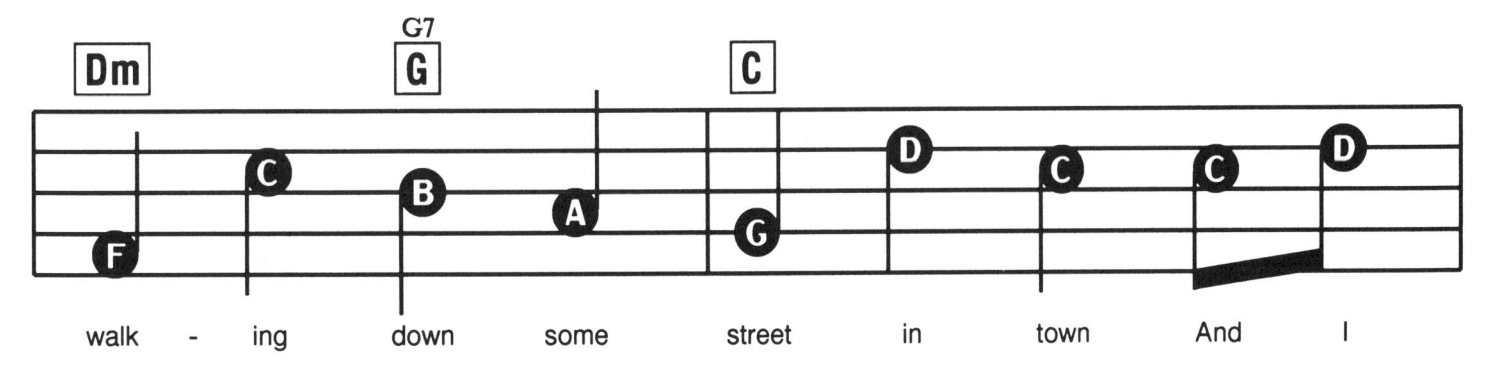

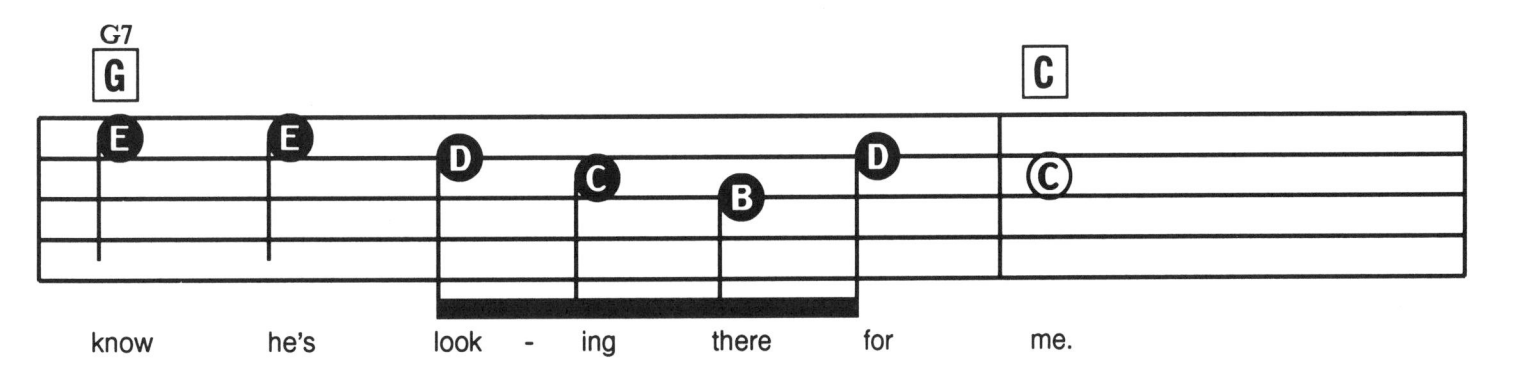

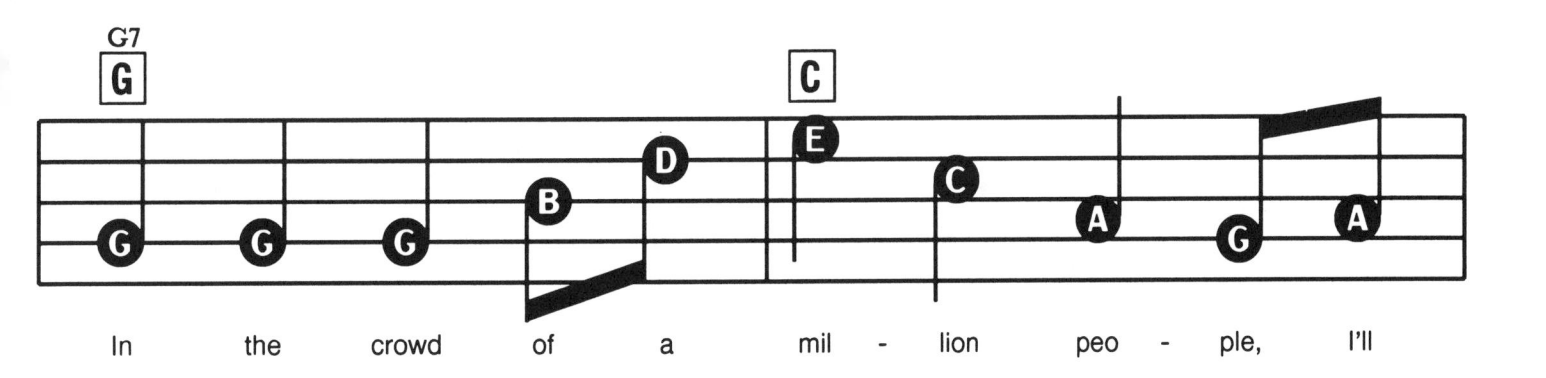

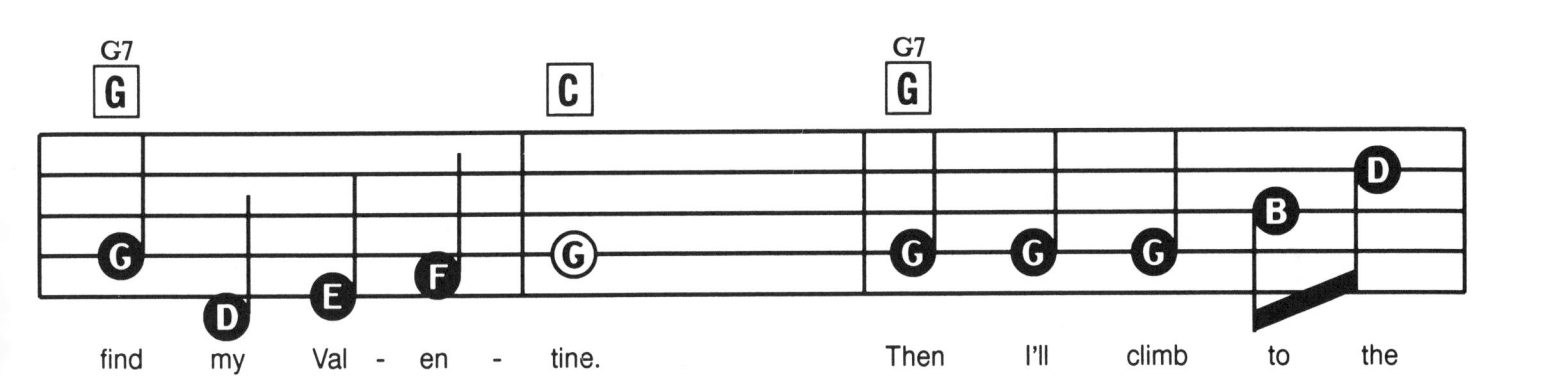

walk - ing down some street in town And I know he's look - ing there for me. In the crowd of a mil - lion peo - ple, I'll find my Val - en - tine. Then I'll climb to the highest steeple And tell the world he's mine. Till he holds me I wait impatiently. Where the boys are, Where the boys are, Where the boys are Someone waits for me.

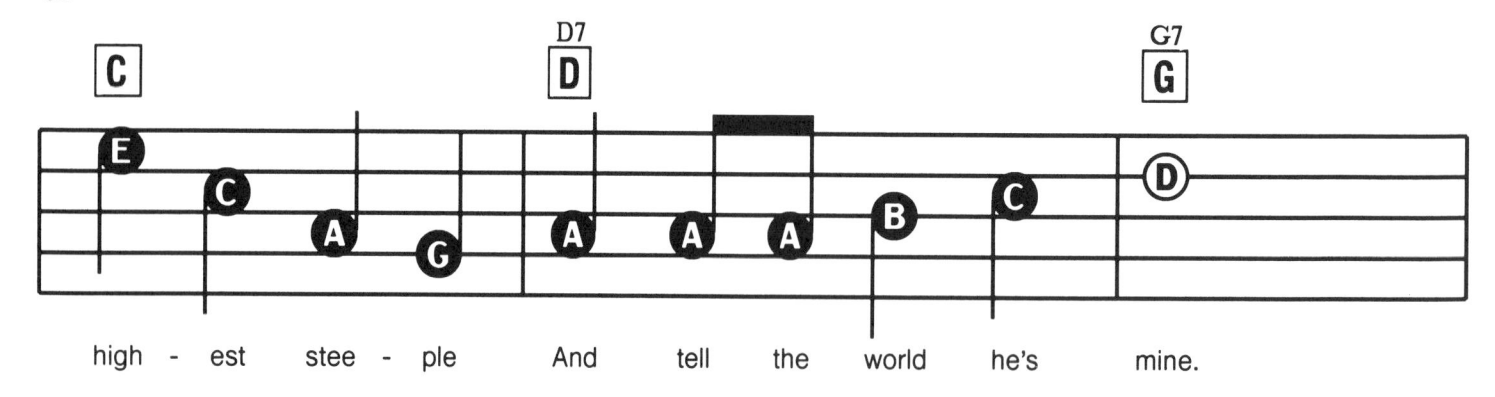

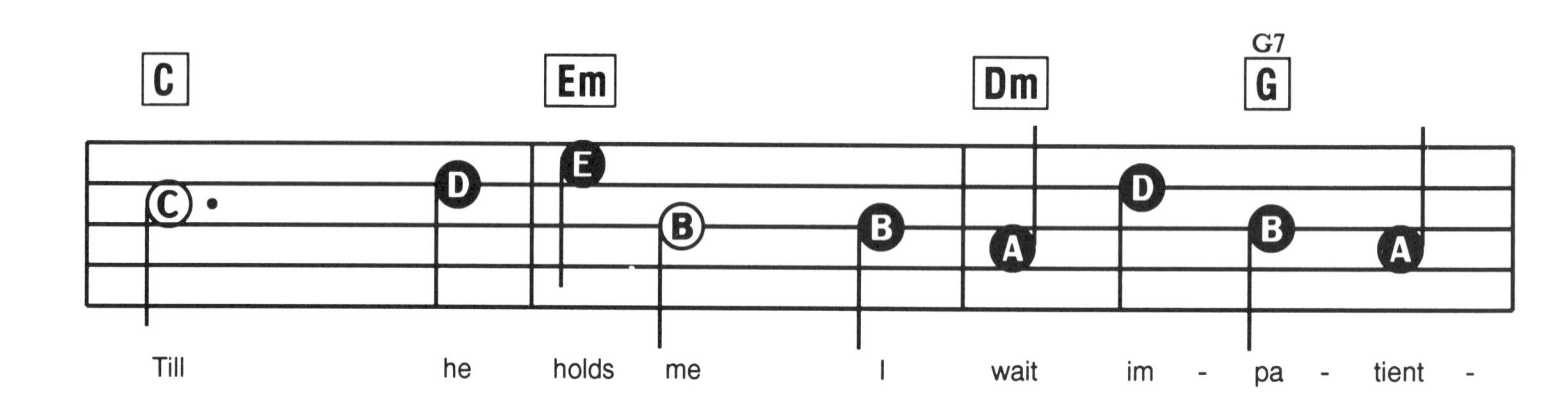

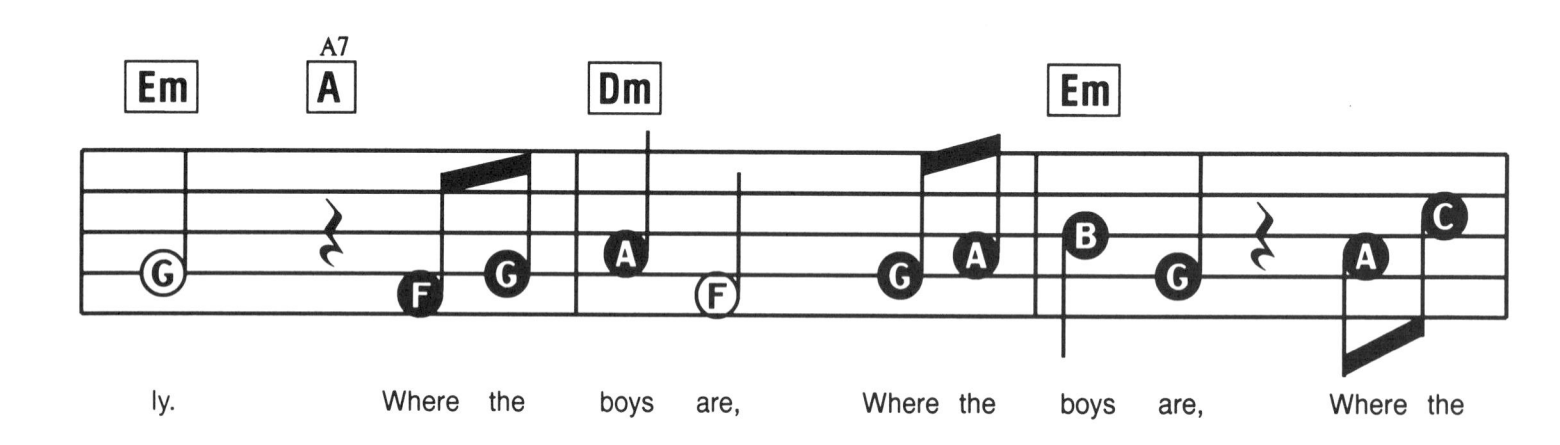

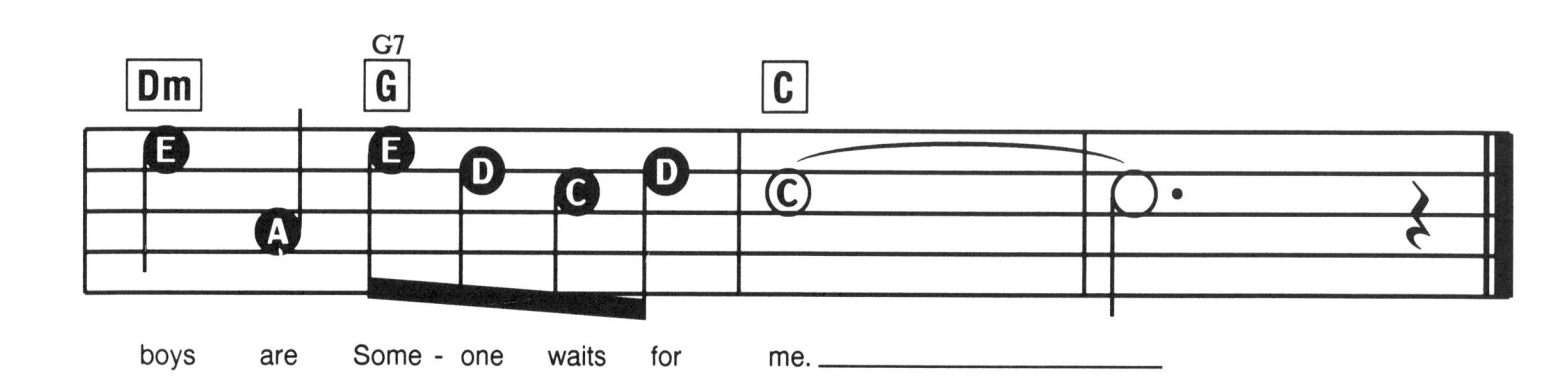

E-Z Play Today Registration Guide

- Match the Registration number on the song to the corresponding numbered category below. Select and activate an instrumental sound available on your instrument.
- Choose an automatic rhythm appropriate to the mood and style of the song. (Consult your Owner's Guide for proper operation of automatic rhythm features.)
- Adjust the tempo and volume controls to comfortable settings.

Registration

1	Mellow	Flutes, Clarinet, Oboe, Flugel Horn, Trombone, French Horn, Organ Flutes
2	Ensemble	Brass Section, Sax Section, Wind Ensemble, Full Organ, Theater Organ
3	Strings	Violin, Viola, Cello, Fiddle, String Ensemble, Pizzicato, Organ Strings
4	Guitars	Acoustic/Electric Guitars, Banjo, Mandolin, Dulcimer, Ukulele, Hawaiian Guitar
5	Mallets	Vibraphone, Marimba, Xylophone, Steel Drums, Bells, Celesta, Chimes
6	Liturgical	Pipe Organ, Hand Bells, Vocal Ensemble, Choir, Organ Flutes
7	Bright	Saxophones, Trumpet, Mute Trumpet, Synth Leads, Jazz/Gospel Organs
8	Piano	Piano, Electric Piano, Honky Tonk Piano, Harpsichord, Clavi
9	Novelty	Melodic Percussion, Wah Trumpet, Synth, Whistle, Kazoo, Perc. Organ
10	Bellows	Accordion, French Accordion, Mussette, Harmonica, Pump Organ, Bagpipes